The Brain

Look for these and other books in the Lucent
Overview series:

Abortion	Homeless Children
Acid Rain	Illegal Immigration
Alcoholism	Illiteracy
Animal Rights	Immigration
Artificial Organs	Mental Illness
The Beginning of Writing	Money
The Brain	Ocean Pollution
Cancer	Oil Spills
Censorship	The Olympic Games
Child Abuse	Organ Transplants
Cities	Ozone
The Collapse of the Soviet Union	Pesticides
Dealing with Death	Police Brutality
Death Penalty	Population
Democracy	Prisons
Drug Abuse	Rainforests
Drugs and Sports	Recycling
Drug Trafficking	The Reunification of Germany
Eating Disorders	Schools
Endangered Species	Smoking
The End of Apartheid in South Africa	Space Exploration
Energy Alternatives	Special Effects in the Movies
Espionage	Teen Alcoholism
Euthanasia	Teen Pregnancy
Extraterrestrial Life	Teen Suicide
Family Violence	The UFO Challenge
Gangs	The United Nations
Garbage	The U.S. Congress
Gay Rights	The U.S. Presidency
The Greenhouse Effect	Vanishing Wetlands
Gun Control	Vietnam
Hate Groups	World Hunger
Hazardous Waste	Zoos
The Holocaust	

The Brain

by Jim Barmeier

LUCENT
BOOKS

LUCENT *Overview Series*

LUCENT *Overview Series*

Library of Congress Cataloging-in-Publication Data

Barmeier, Jim.
    The brain / by Jim Barmeier.
        p.   cm. — (Lucent overview series)
    Includes bibliographical references and index.
    Summary: Explores how the human brain works, covering such topics as memory, sleep, dreaming, dysfunctions, and new technology used to learn more about it.
    ISBN 1-56006-107-3
    1. Brain—Juvenile literature.   2. Neurophysiology—Juvenile literature.   3. Neuropsychology—Juvenile literature.   [1. Brain.] I. Title.   II. Series.
QP376.B353   1996
612.8'2—dc20   95-25183
                                                                  CIP
                                                                   AC

Copyright © 1996 by Lucent Books, Inc.
P.O. Box 289011, San Diego, CA 92198-9011
Printed in the U.S.A.

Contents

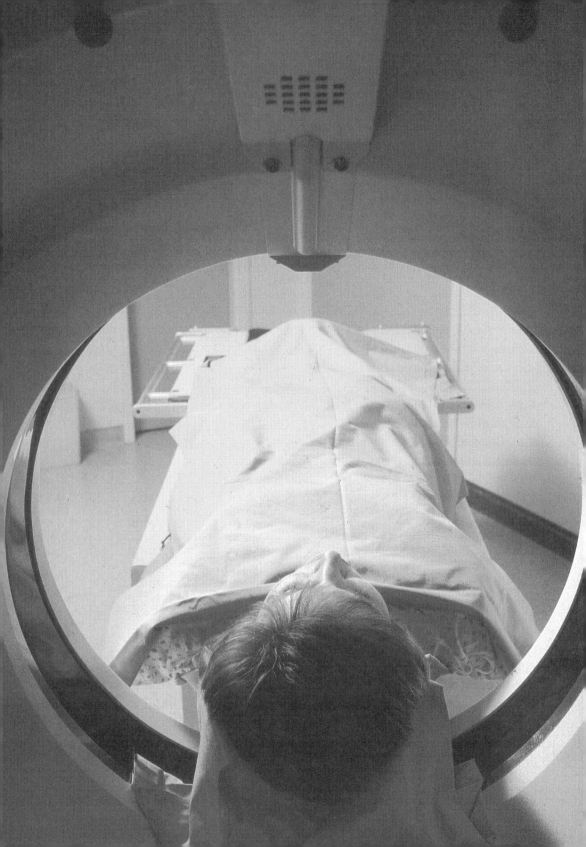

Introduction

THE BRAIN IS the most important organ in the human body. As the control center for all the body's functions, it is the source of everything that a human being does and thinks. Hidden in its curves and bulges are the secrets of intelligence, creativity, memory, emotions, basic instincts, drives, survival, sleeping, and dreaming: in short, the miracle of being human. Sometimes called the most complex matter known to humanity, the brain has been accorded a significance approached by no other organ.

In the last hundred years, scientists have begun to examine the brain and map its functions in ways once believed impossible. They have begun to appreciate how nearly three pounds of intricately interwoven nerve cells can perform its myriad tasks simultaneously twenty-four hours a day. Professor H. Chandler Elliott calls the brain "the climax of a great saga, the tale of a quest for intelligence, for power to achieve and to experience."

Some of the brightest minds in human history have tried to unravel the brain's mysteries. Blocked by the brain's complexity, the slow pace of scientific discovery, and humanity's innate resistance to new ideas and techniques, their progress was slow, their conclusions largely speculative. Despite missteps and dead ends in the quest to un-

(Opposite page) Scientists use tools such as CAT scans to form a picture of how the brain works. Despite huge strides in technology, however, a full understanding of the brain remains elusive.

cover the secrets of the brain, however, modern science owes much to these early explorers.

The history of brain research

Early philosophers and scientists, for the most part, did not recognize the brain's central role in body function and mental and emotional processes. Former senior editor of *Life* magazine Ronald Bailey notes: "For many centuries most men were certain that the seat of behavior was not the brain at all but some other part of the body. The heart was most often singled out as the principal mechanism of human activity."

The Greek philosopher Aristotle, who lived between 384 and 322 B.C., was one who believed that human thoughts and feelings originated in the heart rather than in the brain. He suggested that the brain's main purpose was to cool the blood, basing his conclusions on the mucus of a runny nose. The brain, via the nose, he thought, ventilated the blood with inhaled air and secreted waste in return. The Greek physician Hippocrates, who lived about the time of Aristotle, had a different theory. Considered the founder of modern medicine, Hippocrates correctly concluded that the brain was the center of the senses. However, like most other Greeks of his time, he erroneously believed the brain was powered by changes in the air.

The prevailing explanation of the source of life during this time centered around air. According to this theory, all living things were sustained by air or "pneuma," the Greek word for "soul," or "spirit." Pneuma was responsible for growth, movement, and thought. Making its way to the brain through the liver and heart, it underwent changes on its path through the body. A network of hollow nerve fibers then distributed the pneuma from the brain to the rest of the body.

Called the "father of medicine," the Greek physician Hippocrates correctly theorized that the brain played a central role in bodily functions and behavior.

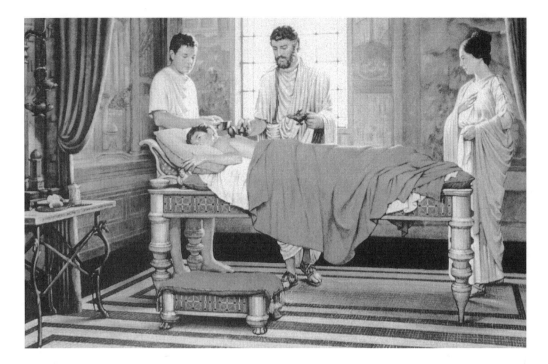

The brain, according to this reasoning, was not as important as the pneuma and, in fact, was secondary in significance to the network that supposedly carried the pneuma through the body.

In the second century A.D., another theory finally elevated the role of the brain. One man, the Greek physician Galen, was responsible. Perhaps the most careful observer of scientific phenomena in ancient times, Galen learned about the structure of the brain by dissecting the heads of animals such as oxen and apes. His research led to his theory that intelligence, sensation, and movement all begin inside cavities of the brain. Galen's ideas did not catch on, however, and the concept of the pneuma—and the lesser role of the brain—prevailed well into the sixteenth century.

The beginnings of modern brain science

By the mid–sixteenth century, Italian medical schools as well as private individuals, artists, and

Galen, a Greek physician who lived in the second century A.D., contributed observations about the physiology of the brain.

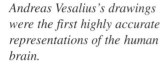

Andreas Vesalius's drawings were the first highly accurate representations of the human brain.

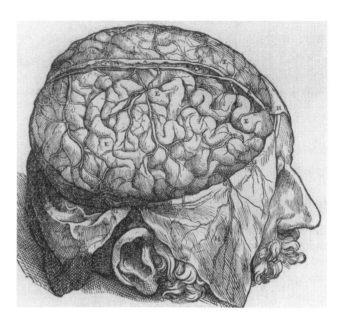

scientists were performing dissections of human cadavers and not merely applying the results of animal dissections to studies of human anatomy and physiology. The illustrations of Andreas Vesalius, made from direct observation of the human brain, precisely depicted details of its structure. Vesalius's drawings, the first accurate descriptions, gave researchers a sound anatomical base for further investigations of the brain.

By the seventeenth century, new techniques for dissecting the brain revealed the complexity of its composition. The brain was no longer described as one solid organ. Instead, it was being revealed, like a jigsaw puzzle, as a collection of related layers, matter, and parts. Although there was still disagreement about the brain's relationship to thought and consciousness, traditional ideas about the brain were being challenged by new explorations.

In the 1660s, one English researcher, Thomas Willis, teamed with inventor and architect Sir Christopher Wren to map the circulation of the blood to the brain. By injecting a special preservative into the blood vessels of animal brains, once invisible blood trails opened up like major highways, demonstrating for the first time how richly supplied with blood all brain tissue is. Early investigators had believed that the most important parts of the brain were the hollow ventricles, which they thought were responsible for memory and reasoning. When it became clear that blood flowed throughout the brain, researchers began to theorize about the roles of previously ignored structures, but lacked the technology to test their theories.

Willis's pioneering efforts were followed up by other brain explorers. German Franciscus Sylvius found indications that the brain's surface, the cortex, was vital to intelligence and thought. He gave his name to the fissure of Sylvius, a deep, narrow

In the seventeenth century, Thomas Willis pioneered studies about blood circulation and the brain. (Left) An illustration of the base of the brain drawn by Willis. (Above) Franciscus Sylvius suggested that the cerebral cortex was a center of intelligence and thought.

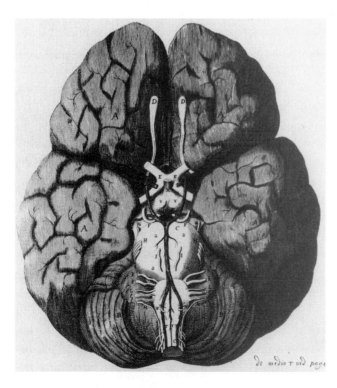

opening in the cortex. Swiss pioneer Albrecht von Haller demonstrated in the 1700s that there was a connection between the cortex and the nerves that led from it to the other body areas. Charles Brown-Sequard of Britain predicted the existence of the chemicals that nerve cells use to transmit messages. Each researcher may have contributed only one small piece of information, but collectively, this information formed a fuller picture of the brain and how it works.

A scientific and technological revolution

None of these revelations would have been possible without the great leaps in scientific technique and technology. Science itself was undergoing a revolution, requiring more rigorous methods and verifiable data in the face of fads and pseudoscience. The scientific revolution was paralleled by incredible improvements in technology. Technical advances, such as the invention of the microscope, led researchers to analyze the brain with greater accuracy. The study of anatomy was made more direct with the development of photography. Photographs of the brain replaced artistic renderings as the staple of neuroscience.

By the second half of the nineteenth century, the contemporary science of the brain was born. With recognition of the human body's complexity came specialization: Among many disciplines related to human biology was now neurology, or the study of the brain and the nervous system. Frenchman Paul Broca found the location for the formation of speech in 1861. Brain damage to that area, he discovered, could affect a person's ability to form words. In 1870, physiologist Eduard Hitzig and zoologist Gustav Fritsch found that the different halves of the brain ruled opposing sides of the body. Capitalizing on their findings, Scotsman David Ferrier mapped the functions of the surface of the halves—the brain's cortex—and how they related to motor skills.

The race to uncover the mysteries of the brain was on. In the words of writer Isaac Asimov, "Not one human being but a scientific team that is scattered over the world is . . . tackling the subject . . . making significant and in some cases astonishing progress."

Throughout the twentieth century, startling technological developments and new research methods have allowed neurologists to systematically begin the tough task of mapping the brain. Since the beginning of this century, neuroscience has racked up an impressive array of accomplishments, including the discovery of the split brain, the location of the brain's emotional centers, the secrets behind sleeping and dreaming, and the chemicals that rule neural behavior. Although scientists agree that the sheer complexity of the brain may make it impossible to completely know this baffling organ, innovative imaging techniques, high-powered computers, scanning, and X-ray machines are the tools a new generation of researchers are using to study the most mysterious organ into the next century.

1

Inside the Brain

WITHIN THE HUMAN BRAIN, which is approximately one-third the size of the human head, buzz billions of nerve cells connected endlessly to other nerve cells, all humming with the activity of human existence. While one part of this neural complex is keeping the body alive, another part may be solving complex math puzzles or writing a speech. Coordination, a beating heart, temperature regulation, sexual attraction—are all controlled by this mass of tissue weighing just three pounds.

The human brain is capable of complex feats, yet it looks like nothing more than a giant soft walnut. Pinkish gray in appearance, it is a puzzle of parts—hills and valleys, bridges and loops, bumps and chambers—all locked into each other. Peeling away each part is a journey back through human evolution: Intricate, uniquely human brain parts sit on top of those commonly shared with the rest of the animal kingdom. It is a grapefruit-size universe of secrets.

What is best known about the brain is its anatomy, the "hardware" of the system. Modern understanding of brain function must begin with a tour of the machinery, starting with the brain's roots at the top of the central nervous system.

Expanding upwards and sideways until it fills the skull, the brain grows from the slender stalk

(Opposite page) Grade school children display their eagerness to solve a math problem. While the human brain resembles nothing more than a giant soft walnut, it controls myriad body processes as well as thought, learning, intelligence, and emotions.

15

of the spinal cord. The brain itself is housed in-side a dome of twenty-two bones that cover one-third of the skull. Sutured together at zigzagging joints, this interlocking connection of calcium is so strong it can protect the brain from all but the strongest impact. The scalp's fatty tissue, the thickest skin on the body, further insulates the convoluted folds from the outside.

Beneath the skull, three membranes wrap around the brain. They cushion it further and lu-bricate its pink-gray tissue. The membrane clos-est to the brain, the pia mater, is rich with blood vessels. Over that is the arachnoid, an elastic web connected to the pia mater. Enclosing both of

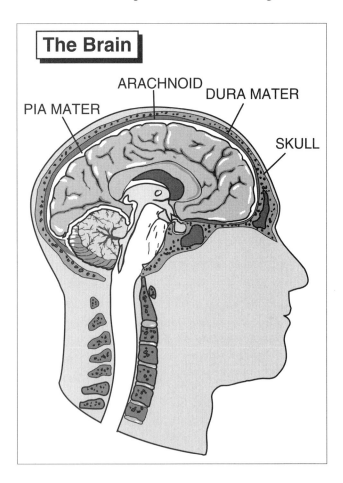

The Brain

PIA MATER

ARACHNOID DURA MATER

SKULL

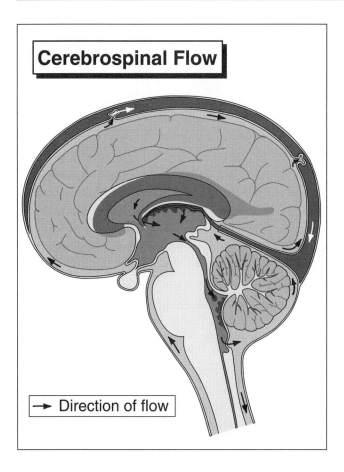

Cerebrospinal Flow

→ Direction of flow

these is a thicker, stronger membrane called the dura mater.

Flowing in and out of its valleys and hills, blood supplies the brain with the oxygen and glucose it cannot hoard. Fully one-fifth of the blood and oxygen used by the body is circulated through the brain. So hungry is it for energy that the brain gulps down more than four hundred calories a day, taken as glucose in the blood.

A second function of the brain's blood supply is to provide the brain with a clear, watery substance called cerebrospinal fluid. Secreted from the blood into the brain's ventricles (the brain's four inner chambers), cerebrospinal fluid cushions the brain and helps maintain a constant pressure within brain and spinal cord tissue. After the fluid fills the ventricles, it travels to the outer surface of the brain. The blood then reabsorbs the fluid and the process repeats.

The parts of the brain

The brain is divided into three main parts, from the oldest (in an evolutionary sense) to the newest. The oldest is the hindbrain, made up of the cerebellum and a big part of the brainstem. The level that developed next is the midbrain, equal to the top of the brainstem. The most recent addition to the human brain is the forebrain, composed of the cerebral hemispheres.

Primitive instincts and automatic responses that all animals share had to develop before the evolution of human thinking and learning. These basics for survival are found in the hindbrain and midbrain.

The hindbrain

More than five hundred million years old in evolutionary terms, and shared with reptiles, birds, and other mammals, the brainstem is the most ancient and lowest part of the brain. It is the center of the body's autonomic, or involuntary, activities, such as balance, breathing and heartbeat, and sleeping and wakefulness. Connected to the spinal cord, the brainstem receives motor and sensory nerve impulses from the body. Less than three inches long, its lower two-thirds is called the hindbrain.

The hindbrain has two main parts: the medulla oblongata and the pons. The fibrous first inch of the brainstem, the medulla is the control center of the brain. It registers injury, monitors blood pressure, and initiates reflex actions like sneezing and laughing. As the link to the spinal cord, the medulla is also the switching station for all the nerve impulses between the body and the brain.

At the point the medulla touches the spinal cord, the majority of nerve fibers from each side of the body cross over to connect to opposing sides of the brain. Here, in the corticospinal decussation, nerves from the left side of the body switch over to the right side of the brain and vice versa. Because of this unusual development, each side of the body is controlled by the opposite side of the brain.

At the back of the medulla rests the reticular formation. No bigger than a thimble, this bundle of fibers and nerve cells is the body's watchdog, alerting the brain for danger. It is also the headquarters for the reticular activating system (RAS). The RAS is deeply involved in the processes of sleeping and wakefulness. Sensory signals pass through this structure. If there is an emergency, the reticular formation activates an alarm in the brain. It stimulates responses from the cortex in the forebrain ranging from waking up to conscious decision making.

Looking like a bridge of white matter and only an inch wide, the pons hangs over the medulla. Bundles of nerve fibers travel between the pons and the cerebellum. One-third of the cranial nerves, considered the most important nerves in the body, arch out from this point. The pons is like a telephone connecting station, attaching the cerebral cortex with the cerebellum.

The cerebellum

Tucked between the cerebral hemispheres and the brainstem, located behind the pons, the cerebellum lords over every activity of the body. Only the cerebrum is larger. The cerebellum accounts for more than 10 percent of the brain's weight and has tripled in size over the last million years. So wrinkled is its surface that only 15 percent of it is visible. Yet special cells on the cerebellum's

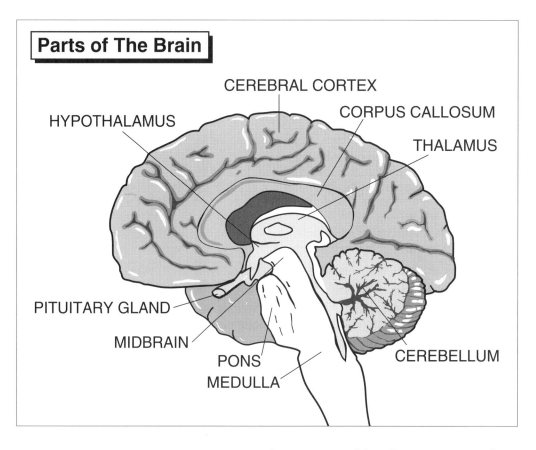

Parts of The Brain

CEREBRAL CORTEX

CORPUS CALLOSUM

HYPOTHALAMUS

THALAMUS

PITUITARY GLAND

MIDBRAIN

PONS

MEDULLA

CEREBELLUM

outer surface are capable of more connections than any other brain cell.

This "little brain," as the cerebellum has been called, doesn't initiate action. Rather, it receives impulses from nerve endings in the inner ear, joints, tendons, and muscles and signals the appropriate body motion, according to orders by the cerebrum in the forebrain. Professor of anatomy H. Chandler Elliott says in *The Shape of Intelligence* that the cerebellum is the reason why "intelligence . . . [switched] from automatic reflexes . . . to free, experimental behavior." In evolutionary terms, coordination and balance were the first functions programmed into the cerebellum. As the "little brain" further evolved, it also took on new responsibilities, including, apparently, memory storage for basic learned responses. Scientists also believe that this structure helps to keep the emotions in harmony.

The midbrain

The smallest of the three parts of the brain, the midbrain is located at the top of the brainstem. No longer than a fingertip, it is, like the pons, a connecting station of nerve fibers and nuclei for sensory signals entering from one location and moving on to the next. In *The Brain*, Dr. Richard Restak states that "elementary forms of seeing or hearing are possible in the midbrain."

As human beings evolved, their needs advanced beyond simply seeing or hearing or smelling or achieving two-legged balance. What was fine for primitive animals no longer met more sophisticated challenges. The forebrain, the home of the thinking cerebrum and the source of humankind's unique characteristics, is the most recent addition to the architecture of the brain.

The forebrain

The forebrain comprises five structures essential to human body function: the limbic system, the hypothalamus, the thalamus, the basal ganglia, and the cerebrum.

In reptiles, the limbic system was used primarily to help a creature smell what was around it. It dominated the forebrain. In human beings, smelling is not so necessary for daily survival, and the limbic system's dominance has been overshadowed by the cerebrum's. In fact, this area used to be called the rhinencephalon, or "smell brain," until it was given its current name, which means "bordering system."

Located right above the brainstem in the center of the brain, the limbic system appeared at least two hundred million years ago, and today looks like a complex of curved objects encircling the top of the brainstem like a wishbone. It comprises the sea horse–shaped hippocampus, the almond-shaped amygdala, the hypothalamus, and the thalamus. Scientists made revolutionary strides in understanding the limbic system when they started to probe the cells of living subjects with microscopic electrodes and noted the reaction. Because the brain has no nerve cells to feel pain, it can be probed without anesthetic. Experimenting first on the brains of lab animals, researchers discovered that exciting certain sites on the limbic system with a low-voltage electrical stimulus elicited sudden fear, excitement, or rage. Interestingly, when the same cells were stimulated repeatedly, an entirely different emotion might be triggered, leading scientists to believe that no one group of cells in the limbic system was assigned any particular emotion.

The emotions generated in the limbic system have to do with survival: fight-or-flight urges and sexual desire. Scientists also know that the limbic system is responsible for maintaining internal stability by regulating heart rate, blood pressure, body temperature, and blood sugar levels. One way a warm-blooded, mammalian human being is distinguished from a cold-blooded creature is because of the limbic system. It helps us to adjust our internal environment to keep it constant, regardless of conditions in the outside climate. The limbic system is also an automatic pilot for the body; it will continue to maintain vital bodily functions with the aid of the brainstem even if a person is comatose.

The centers of the brain

Deep down between the brainstem and the cerebral hemispheres are the thalamus and the hypothalamus, the brain's primary interconnectors of all the nerve impulses from the senses to the cerebral cortex. Everything a human perceives through sight, smell, touch, and taste filters through these structures. Both egg-shaped in appearance, the thalami are clusters of gray matter.

Some experts consider the hypothalamus to be the most fascinating area of the brain. Although only the size of the tip of a thumb, it can do more per unit of weight (it weighs only four grams) than any other part of the brain. As the control booth for the limbic system, it is the middleman between the brain and the body. Sharing the responsibility of regulating vital bodily functions with the rest of the limbic system, the hypothalamus monitors sexual drive, hunger, thirst, sleeping and waking, hormone and chemical balances, basic emotions, and body temperature. "[It] is directly responsible for innate biological drives that are most fundamental to survival," says Ronald Bailey in *The Role of the Brain*, "those that keep the body supplied with the warmth and energy essential to life." The hypothalamus does its job by reacting to sensory input, like a smoke alarm responds to smoke. If the body is overheating, for example, the hypothalamus triggers the cooling mechanisms of the body, opening the sweat glands.

"Brain within the brain"

That's not the only job of this "brain within the brain." Production of hormones, the chemical substances that stimulate body activity, is also influenced by the hypothalamus. The master gland for all hormones, the pituitary, is directed by this limbic boss. Using electrical and chemical impulses to communicate, the hypothalamus oversees the pituitary, which in turn combines many of the hormones that are used as messengers to other glands of the body. Special nerve cells in the brain pro-

When the body overheats, as it does during strenuous exercise, the hypothalamus triggers the body's cooling mechanisms, which includes opening the sweat glands.

duce these chemical hormones, which affect such activities as growth and sexual interest.

The counterpart of the pituitary gland is the pineal gland. Cone-shaped in appearance and located at the base of the brain, the pineal gland regulates the body's biological clock, monitoring data about light and dark recorded by the senses. Such cyclic activities as sleeping, waking, and menstruation are affected by this gland, as is the onset of puberty. So finely developed is the pineal that even a person confined to a dark cave could still generally keep accurate time.

Right in the center of the forebrain is the thalamus. Acting somewhat like a central train station, it switches every signal from the sensory organs except smell to the cortex, the "thinking cap" of the brain. The different parts of the thalamus are specialized to process different types of sensory data, which are then relayed on to those parts of the cortex that govern specialized activity.

"Smell . . . has its own private connection to the higher centers, an inch-long olfactory bulb that juts forward from the base of each cerebral hemisphere and carries the news from the nose directly to the brain," writes Ronald Bailey in *The Role of the Brain*. "This mainline connection, which is unique among the body's senses, may explain the extraordinary ability of odors to evoke some of the most powerful of human memories."

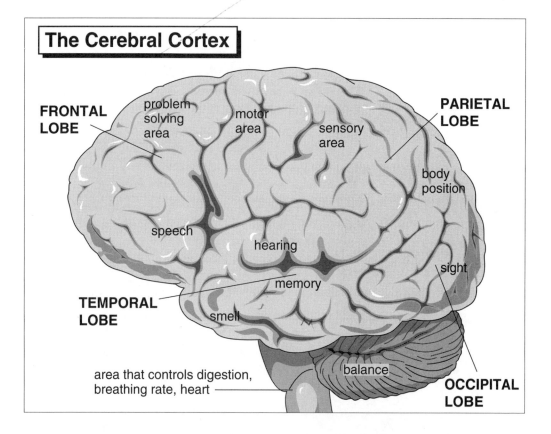

The Cerebral Cortex

FRONTAL LOBE

problem solving area

motor area

sensory area

PARIETAL LOBE

body position

speech

hearing

sight

TEMPORAL LOBE

memory

smell

area that controls digestion, breathing rate, heart

balance

OCCIPITAL LOBE

Paired on either side of the limbic system are the basal ganglia. Looking like large clusters of nerve cells, they assist in helping the body coordinate its physical movements. When a person lifts a leg, extends an arm, or turns the neck, to name a few activities, the basal ganglia have initiated that action.

All of the parts of the forebrain are very important to the functioning of the body. But all of the other structures are subordinate to and work in connection with the cerebral cortex—the newest part, the one that makes a creature distinctively human.

The newest part of the brain

Wrinkled like a walnut, the cerebrum covers the other areas of the brain like a spongy helmet. Its higher functions are the subject of the most advanced studies in neuroscience. The wrinkles of the cerebrum twist and turn with no apparent pattern, packed with more nerve cells than in any other part of the brain. "Here evolution added all the gadgetry that distinguishes man from the lizard, so it is not surprising that in humans the cerebrum is an overfed giant," Judith Hooper and Dick Teresi state in *Three-Pound Universe.* Scientists know that the cerebrum handles thinking and some types of memory, but they still don't know precisely how either one works.

What they do know is that the cerebrum is divided into two hemispheres, or halves, separated vertically. Each half might appear to be a mirror image of the other but in actuality the symmetry is anatomical, not functional. The right hemisphere controls the left side of the body; the left hemisphere controls the right, and each half plays a unique role in personality and development.

Why each half of the brain controls its opposite body side, or even why there are two halves, is not known. "Accordingly to one theory," writes Richard Restak in *The Brain*, "the two hemispheres provide backup systems for each other in the event of damage to one."

The cortex

Covering the surface of the hemispheres, the tissue that gives the cerebrum its wrinkled appearance is the cortex. Although it's less than a quarter-inch thick, its total surface area is around two and a half square feet, each cubic inch composed of six distinct layers of cells. From outermost to innermost, they are the outer molecular layer, the external granular layer, the outer pyramidal layer, the internal granular layer, the ganglionic layer, and the multiform layer.

Restak summarizes the conclusions of brain researchers on the subject: "The cerebral cortex furnishes us with our most human qualities: our language, our ability to reason, to deal with symbols, and to develop a culture." Only mammals have a true cortex, which allows more complex mental activities than reflex reactions and instincts. And no mammal except human beings has such an intricately folded cerebral surface, stretching over and around the rest of the brain. Some scientists have theorized that the folding has evolved to enable an organ capable of advanced functioning to fit in an infant-size skull.

Porridgelike in appearance, the cortex lacks rhyme or reason in the pattern of its cells and fibers. Scientists know that the cortex is responsible for information processing: receiving, analyzing, comparing, recording, and making decisions. But how the cortex does this is still open to theory.

Brain researchers have mapped some of the specialized parts of the cortex, dividing it into four regions called lobes. The occipital lobe, temporal lobe, frontal lobe, and parietal lobe form the cortex. The lobes are further designated as right or left, as each is a region of both hemispheres.

The lobes of the cortex

At the back of the head is the occipital lobe. The home of the main visual area in the brain, it is critical to the analysis of visual information received by the eyes. Disease in or damage to this area can render a person totally or partially blind, even though the eyes may be completely healthy. Scientists found out much about the occipital lobe from examining brain wounds during World Wars I and II.

Near the temples are the temporal lobes. Unlike the occipital, the temporal lobes have several jobs. One important responsibility is to process acoustic stimuli, i.e., hearing. This is the auditory cortex. Other functions are associated with per-

A photograph of a healthy human brain clearly shows the wrinkled, folded cerebral cortex.

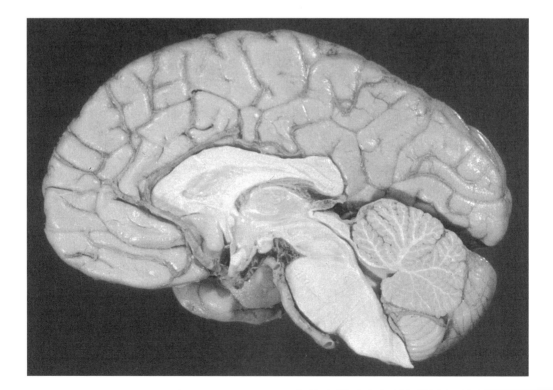

ception and memory. Also, some visual communications that have already been analyzed by the occipital lobe are transferred to the temporal lobe under certain conditions.

Damage to the temporal lobes produces a fascinating range of effects. Sometimes, people cannot remember any events that happen after an injury is sustained. Others may suffer from hallucinations and bizarre sensations. When the lobes are stimulated electrically, different reactions occur. Subjects may feel as if they are in two places at once; the past may mix with the present in memory; weird emotions spring up out of nowhere. The unfamiliar may seem familiar and vice versa. Stroke victims whose temporal lobes are heavily damaged can no longer talk intelligibly. If just the right temporal lobe is damaged, by comparison, such spatial abilities as drawing may be handicapped.

The parietal lobes, located at the top and rear of the brain, control two distinct types of body activity: the awareness of and the movements of the body. Injury to the parietal lobes may leave a person in a state of "not knowing": He or she may not recognize or even ignore what was previously familiar, like a part of their body. A person with this condition, for instance, may only wash half of his body, literally unconscious of the other half.

The largest lobe

Immediately behind the forehead is the frontal lobe. The biggest of all the lobes, it monitors many of the emotional and decision-making activities of the brain. Whatever is not governed by the other lobes is probably overseen by the frontal. Some experts have even argued that the abilities of the frontal cortex are what make a person distinctively human. The capacities to be spontaneous and adaptive, to plan ahead and carry out activities, and to act purposefully are frontal lobe responsibilities. Without this lobe, human beings become distracted by trivia, don't care, are unaware of their surroundings, cannot think ahead, and develop an emotionally flat personality.

In a famous case, a twenty-five-year-old man named Phineas Gage was the victim of an awful accident in 1848. A large metal rod was driven through his head by an explosion. Although the rod was removed successfully and Gage appeared to be normal, in a way he was not. The rod had pierced his frontal cortex. Once intelligent and organized, he was transformed into an irresponsible, swearing loafer. As Restak points out in *The Brain*, "His injury and the effects it had on his personality provided the first clear indication of the delicate physical balance within the brain between thought and emotion."

Prefrontal lobotomy

A once highly popular operation called prefrontal lobotomy was performed to treat several types of mental illness. The nerve fibers between the lobe and the rest of the brain were cut, turning patients into emotional vegetables. Author Anthony Smith describes the origins of this psychosurgery in *The Mind*. "[It] began in 1935 when Egon Moniz, Portuguese neurologist, severed the frontal lobes of four depressed, paranoid schizophrenics. Their original symptoms were relieved, but replaced by nausea and disorientation. . . . Others took up the scalpel where he had pioneered, and by 1951 over eighteen thousand Americans—the depressed, violent, schizophrenic, and alcoholic—had been lobotomized." Widely used on aggressive behavior in the 1940s and 1950s, prefrontal lobotomy has since fallen into disfavor.

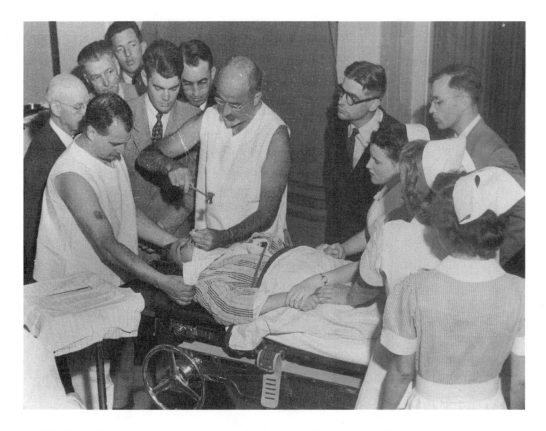

A medical team performs a prefrontal lobotomy in 1949. To sever the frontal lobes of the patient's brain, the doctor inserts a cutting instrument through the patient's upper eyelid.

Without the nervous system, the brain could be likened to a computer's central processing unit that is turned off. The nervous system connects the brain with the muscles and sense endings, like wires that hook up to the master control. Signals feed into the system; responses are returned. The body's neurons transmit messages to one another through electrical and chemical impulses. Most neurons—the basic unit by which the brain processes information—are no larger than a millionth of a yard.

Two types of nerve matter compose the brain. The gray matter is nerve cells. The white matter is nerve fibers, wrapped in a white, fatty, insulating material. The nerve fibers are categorized according to origin and brain destination. Each neuron is part of a circuit of neurons, communicating through an interweaving of short fibers. Each neuron can be divided into three parts: the cell body, axon, and dendrites. Like other body cells, a neuron has a cell body, composed of a nucleus sheathed by a sticky fluid. The power of the neurons is in their axon and dendrites, which have become specialized to conduct information. The axon is a long stem that grows out of the cell. The point where axons connect is named a synapse; it is at the synapse that neurons communicate with each other. The brain is always firing with these communications, bombarding any one cell with thousands of conflicting signals. Given the number of nerve cells in the brain, the number of conceivable synaptic connections between

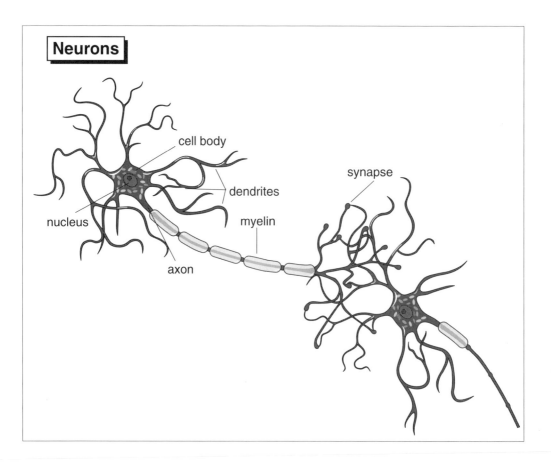

Neurons

cell body

synapse

dendrites

nucleus

myelin

axon

neurons is practically infinite. Only nerve cells and the cells they are communicating with have these synapses. Only the neuron's information processing ability keeps the right signal going on the right path. All the rest of the fibers leaving the cell are dendrites, best described as information receivers.

A cross section of the human brain looks like a disorganized mass of cells. Indeed, until the twentieth century many scientists felt that the brain was a continuous tissue, not composed of individual cells. It was not until an Italian anatomist, Camillo Golgi, devised a unique stain that would highlight nerve cells that neurologists started to believe differently. In the late 1880s, leapfrogging on Golgi's discovery, another researcher, Santiago Ramón y Cajal, used Golgi's method to prove the individual cell theory. The fact that all of these cells' signals are transmitted correctly is amazing. A means of wiring known only to the brain makes sure that a message to the eye, for instance, does not get sidetracked to the left knee. The design and refinements of this wiring are shaped by growth and experience throughout a lifetime.

What is known today about the inside of the brain is the result of decades of hard work, scientific discovery, pure accident, individual accomplishment, and strong teamwork. Part of the brain's map has been drawn so far. But there is still much to be done. Scientists are continually amazed about what they discover about the inside of the brain—its shape, its hemispheres, its parts, its cells—and the discovery continues.

Italian anatomist Camillo Golgi used a stain to highlight nerve cells in his pioneering brain research.

2
Memory

IN THE RELATIVELY long course of a human lifetime, the one connection between the events of childhood and a moment in old age is memory. Memory is what gives a human being personal identity—what tells a person who he or she is—and links yesterday to today.

Every day the brain decides which of thousands of experiences to commit to this vast warehouse, how to process them, which to destroy or detain in short- or long-term memory. Without memory, there would be no past, no recollections of childhood, no ability to retain even a telephone number heard a moment ago. Without memory, every event, person, and moment would be brand new, even if each had been repeated a thousand times. The reader could recall nothing prior to this sentence.

In ancient times, a good memory was vital to survival and achievement. Before the development of written language and the printed word, the memory was the only storehouse of human knowledge. Even after the development of writing, ancient scholars memorized hundreds, if not thousands, of handwritten pages of great works to pass on to succeeding generations in case the originals were lost. Thus, memory contained the heritage of human history.

(Opposite page) To this elderly couple, a photograph triggers happy recollections of a past event. Without memory, there could be no past, no link between one moment and the next.

It's hard to imagine not having any kind of memory. Without this ability of the brain, one moment would be unconnected to the next. What's more, the memory is the guardian for the brain. It educates, warns, alerts, and monitors. It is the watchdog against mistakes and the reservoir for all the facts one needs to survive. Yet there are those who, either through injury or disease, have incomplete warehouses of memories.

In the ongoing investigations of neuroscience, researchers have learned that memory is of various types, that it is found in several locations, and that probably it is even stored in the brain in some kind of biological code. But exactly what that code is or how it got there or how memory is formed is still open to debate.

Much of that investigation depends on what type of memory science is talking about. Remembering a grocery list is different from remembering one's name. Recognizing a face is different from recalling a favorite musical tune. The two most widely accepted types of memory are short-term and long-term, categories that are defined by the length of time a piece of information is kept in the brain.

Short-term memory

Short-term memory starts with the stimulus that triggers the senses, say the vision of a bird. Awareness has started. The eye sees something: a flash of wings. A warble is picked up by the ear. In the split second that the senses register this piece of information, the brain keeps it on hold. For an instant, as the experience flows in, the stimulus rests in what could be described as the sensory register. This register holds an image just long enough for the brain to decide how to handle it. A visual image is retained for one second, a sound for four seconds or less.

Most experience perceived by the senses is discarded immediately by the brain, even before it reaches consciousness. A person's ability to focus on information limits what kind of data are filtered in. Once the brain decides to accept the experience, the image passes into short-term memory. Short-term memory can best be described as a memory waiting room. Scientists disagree as to just how long it lasts. Although the brain is constantly erasing and letting in information, short-term memory only endures from one minute to several days, depending on whether new data has been deleted or rehearsed.

Research has shown that an average of only six or seven chunks of information (like a license plate number) can be retained at any one time in short-term memory. A chunk can be anything from a single number to a group of commonly related data—like a phone number. The brain keeps this information as coded sounds, i.e., language, if possible, with visual images accounting for the rest.

A significant amount of what neuroscience knows about short-term memory has come from brain surgery. In this process, surgeons have discovered that short-term memory might be localized in a tiny section of the left hemisphere's cerebral cortex. In one experiment, brain patients under local anesthesia, and thus able to talk, were having their cerebral cortex explored with an electrical stimulus to locate diseased brain tissue. When the stimulus temporarily numbed a small portion of the cortex, the doctors accidentally found that short-term memory was also temporarily inactivated.

Long-term memory

If a special effort is made to remember information—for example, a phone number—that piece of data shifts into long-term memory. Here's how it works. Once attention is focused on something—say someone wants to remember the name of a person they just met—the brain selectively blocks any other experiences or data from being admitted into short-term memory. Nor will the brain let that important bit of information be erased while it's being rehearsed. If this information is repeated and thought about long enough, it passes into permanent memory.

Data in long-term memory can also be forgotten, but not quite the same way as with short-term memory. The more important the information and/or the better it is organized as it is filed into the memory, the less likely it will be forgotten. Once in long-term memory, items can be retained for a lifetime.

The permanent, long-term memory can store an amazing amount of information. Some scien-

Data passes into permanent memory when a special effort is made to focus attention and remember information.

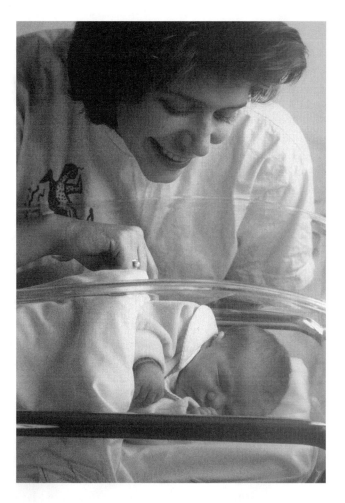

tists believe its capacity is almost unlimited. All the experience of a lifetime, millions of "bits" of information, have the potential of being stored here. So durable is permanent memory that this type of information is well protected by the brain. Electrical shock, drugs, and other kinds of blows will usually not destroy it permanently. "Even a blow to the head severe enough to cause amnesia," writes Ronald Bailey, "may not destroy [it]." Amnesia is a loss of memory due to brain injury, shock, fatigue, repression, or illness.

Because this type of memory is more complex than short-term memory, scientists believe that

Knowing how to drive a car is an example of procedural memory. Stopping at a red light, however, is stimulus response memory.

the way it retains information is also more sophisticated. One of the most popular theories is that the strongest memories are those that are charged with the highest emotions. This means that the emotional centers of the brain might determine the durability of a memory. The most important part is probably the hippocampus, a small, sea horse–shaped chunk of tissue located under each temporal lobe—because it intensifies emotional images on the brain, something like getting a higher quality photographic print.

Confirmation of this idea has come in cases where the hippocampus has been damaged. In these situations, the brain seems unable to keep long-term memories. The most famous case was a person known to science as H. M. In 1953, he had surgery at the Montreal Neurological Institute to relieve his severe epilepsy. The procedure was on his temporal lobes, but it accidentally injured his hippocampus. Interestingly, the patient could remember nothing after his operation; his memory span was about fifteen minutes. But everything before his operation was crystal clear. Each time he met someone or did something after the operation, even if he had done it before, it was as though it were for the first time.

Other types of memory

The two types of memory are subdivided into a host of other specialties which are classified according to the type of information stored. "Procedural memory" recalls experiences useful in knowing how to do something, such as driving a car. "Stimulus response memory" will make a person instinctively react to a stimulus—for instance, stop at a red light. "Event memory" handles special situations, places, and times. It is one of the types of memory most likely to decline with old age. "Semantic memory" is concerned with ideas, language, and facts. Unlike the previous memory type, it seems to be resistant to aging. The biggest warehouse of knowledge is called "abstract memory," which governs the meaning of things. Knowing how to turn on a TV would be procedural memory; knowing what a TV does would be abstract memory.

Research is continuing into how the brain remembers. Some memories are associated with sounds, like language, which has a definite location in the left hemisphere. Other memories are more visual and are also associated with those locations in the brain that handle pictures. But what has eluded scientists is the big picture: knowing how all memories are formed and where they are stored. Authors Judith Hooper and Dick Teresi write in *The Three-Pound Universe* that "if scientists can ever turn up an exact correspondence between a group of neurons and the memory of your first communion, we would be close to knowing how three pounds of wet tissue can house a mind."

The search for the source of memory

Unlike other abilities of the brain, like emotions or language, so far science has been unable to find any specific home for memory. Emotions are in the limbic system and language is in the left hemisphere, but the headquarters for storage and recall has been elusive. Just as one scientist believes that he or she has found the source, another comes along to debunk it. The engram, after the Greek word for "trace," is what science calls this basic home for memory. If the memory detectives can just find this mysterious location, they might be able to understand how a soggy lump of nerve cells can contain the experiences of a lifetime.

The guiding force behind the memory trackers was American neuropsychologist Karl Lashley. Starting in the 1920s, Lashley attempted to pinpoint the exact location of memory in the brains of his animal subjects. For thirty years, Lashley taught rats how to respond to maze experiments, then surgically removed different parts of their brain surfaces. He reasoned that at some point he would cut out that part of memory that governs maze-running ability. Much to his surprise, that did not happen. In fact, even though he retested the same rats on the same maze, some with big chunks of their cortex removed, the undaunted rats still managed to stumble through the experiments. Neither the amount removed nor the location made any difference. Though other abilities might be affected as he cut away, Lashley could never fully eliminate the memory of the rats. Disappointed at not achieving his lifelong goal, Lashley decided that, in contrast to other cerebral abilities, memory could be found everywhere in the brain, not in one special place. His 1950 paper entitled "In Search of the Engram," published at the end of his career, stated that "there is no great excess of cells which can be reserved as the seat of special memories."

Clues to memory

By sheer coincidence, Canadian neurosurgeon Wilder Penfield was examining the brains of epileptics about the time that Lashley made his conclusions. He was using electrical stimulation on the brains of epileptic patients to see where they had been damaged. They talked to Penfield while he selectively examined their cortex. When he touched the temporal lobes, specifically that area connected to the limbic system, the reaction was surprising. The patients started giving very detailed and even emotional responses, recalling events from the past. Sounds, tastes, and sights filtered in and out of their memory. One young boy remembered a long-lost relative as if he were right there in the room. Another could repeat a piece of music, note for note.

Patient after patient, forty in all, recalled vivid details of their lives, just in response to the probe. The conversation of the young boy mentioned above is recalled in *The Role of the Brain*: "'Oh, gosh!' exclaims one 12-year-old boy, 'There they are, my brother is there. He is aiming an air rifle at me.'" Penfield believed that the patients had relived an earlier experience through flashbacks and that the temporal lobes connected the cortex to the brain's deeper brain structures. Even more amazing, he deduced that the brain stores all the information of a lifetime, like a vast encyclopedia of trivia. His patients, time after time, experienced these memories in brief bursts, but they could not consciously recall them. What's more, the memories were revealed like scenes in a

Canadian neurosurgeon Wilder Penfield provided new information about memory during experiments in which he electrically stimulated the cortex of epileptic patients.

movie, as they actually happened, and not as if the brain had organized them.

Penfield concluded that he had found the engram or at least one location for memory in the brain. It was a startling discovery, but not long-lived. Other researchers claimed that it was not the temporal lobes that Penfield touched, but the limbic system, which has been linked with memory formation. Nonepileptic people, they pointed out, when stimulated don't experience these flashbacks. Thinking back to Lashley, Penfield's critics thought that maybe the neural code for memory is repeated throughout the cortex, as a backup in case one code is destroyed, or that codes throughout the brain can be aroused from stimulating certain areas. These were only theories, and they still don't explain why some memories (like those of prespeech infancy) can't be recalled or why a single stimulus, like a smell, can unleash a whole flood of memories.

Finding a location for memory

Despite some research to the contrary, some neuroscientists still hold to the belief that memory has a specific location. After all, if other types of behavior have a home in the brain, shouldn't memory?

Finding a location for memory would solve part of the problem for neuroscience, but the investigation would also have to continue into the basic issue: How does the brain make a memory?

Some of the answers may be linked to whether the brain is forming a short- or a long-term memory. Canadian psychologist Donald Hebb, in what has become one of the reigning theories today, saw the two types of memory as differences in the organization of nerve cells. When a nerve cell is required to learn some new information—a bit of data—the connections or synapses between it and other relevant cells are strengthened or altered. The nerve cells fire from the stimulus of this new data, forming a pattern. In short-term memory, the pattern freezes just long enough to retain this information temporarily. The impulse that creates this short-lived pattern is thought to be electrical, so as not to permanently affect the brain. To become a long-term memory, the impulse, it is believed, actually has to physically change the brain, like a flow of water that cuts into a riverbed. This microscopic change in the anatomy of the brain would be the elusive engram that Lashley and Penfield were investigating.

Aplysia provides clues to memory

Hebb's theory has been supported by research on one of the most primitive animals in existence, the giant sea slug, *Aplysia*. This foot-long animal has large nerve cells, big enough to be penetrated by electricity-measuring microelectrodes. From the 1960s to the 1980s, subjecting this slug to a variety of learning tests, neuroscientist Eric Kandel discovered that *Aplysia*'s nerve cells altered as they learned. The alteration had to do with changes at the nerve endings, at the synapse. The physical structure actually changed, presumably through neurochemicals. Although science isn't completely sure that the human brain works the same way as a simple slug, the prevailing conclusion is that learning involves changes in the ways that nerves send and receive information.

For a memory to become permanent within the brain, to become so solid that not even a blow to the head would destroy it, the brain must change structurally and biochemically. The memory must be part of the brain and not just a ghost floating through it. The explanations for this development are both interesting and controversial.

Researchers started looking at one of the basic building blocks of living matter, protein. Because nerve cells make and process more protein than any other type of body cell, protein molecules, it was thought, had a specific purpose inside the brain, maybe even memory. This assumed that memories are encoded biochemically in the brain. Since the sixties, experiments with rats, chickens, and goldfish seemed to verify this theory. After looking at the neurons of laboratory animals when they learned something, investigators found a buildup of RNA, or ribonucleic acid. A protein builder, RNA is important to sending genetic messages. Preventing or increasing the production of RNA seems to affect learning. Taking this one step further, researcher Georges Unger suggested that any number of compounds or biochemicals, not just protein or RNA, could be linked to memory. In fact, a specific chemical might be used by the brain to both encode and trigger each and every ability it learns.

Memory transfer research

If the type of memory building block was found and located, some investigators reasoned, wouldn't it be possible to isolate this storage unit, cut it out, and transfer it to another animal, like a skin graft or organ transplant? If that were possible, then one person's memories could be implanted in another. All scientists had to do was find that molecule or group of molecules that held, say, a musical score or baseball trivia and implant it in another to prove their theory.

The easiest way to test this was by training an animal to learn a new skill, then removing pieces of its brain and surgically grafting them to a similar animal to see if the knowledge would be transferred. One of the more controversial examples of this memory transfer research was the flatworm experiments of psychologist James McConnell in the 1960s. McConnell sliced up the bodies of worms he had trained to respond to light and fed them to untrained worms. The scientist claimed that the fed worms actually duplicated the trained behavior of their brethren, thus supporting the theory. No other researcher anywhere, however, could duplicate McConnell's results. Furthermore, as Ronald Bailey says: "In an unusual step, 23 scientists wrote to the magazine *Science* announcing that none had been able to duplicate the [learning transfer] experiment [of one of McConnell's associates, Allan Jacobson.]" Georges Unger also made similar claims, also discounted, with a memory molecule he felt held the code for a fear of darkness.

"Memory transfer" inspired the science fiction idea that knowledge could be swallowed like a vitamin. If one collected the right molecules, it might be possible to eat your way to an encyclopedia of memory. The whole concept fell out of favor by the end of the 1960s, though, as critics poked holes in its logic.

What was important in the understanding of memory went beyond memory transfer. It was an appreciation not only of how memory was formed and where it was located, but also how the brain retrieved information it had stored.

Recalling and forgetting

Obviously, the brain must organize information in a way that makes recall possible. Some information is stored as raw, unconnected data; some may be woven into a record that may be accurate or it may be embellished, hazy, or false. Regardless, each person has his or her own particular capacities for recall. Children often have so-called photographic memories, probably because they record things early as images and not words, but this ability seems to decline with age. Having an accurate, highly recallable memory is prized by many. World records exist of people who have memorized thousands of pages of text.

However, the human memory is not infallible. It can blank out or simply not recall accurate information. Why the brain may give false memories is open to debate. Scientists believe the brain uses clues to cross-reference the information it receives. Sometimes these clues are obvious: A grocery list will remind a person what to buy. Sometimes they are less direct: The smell associated with eating a bowl of soup can recall a happy vacation. Sights, sounds, smells, every plausible or implausible clue can link the present with the past. In a moment, the brain processes myriad mazes of electrical or biochemically coded memories to find the appropriate thought. The recall can be brought up at will, through an appropriate tag (for example, a letter can be a memory tag for someone's name), unconsciously, or even by surprise. A hypnotist can bring up memories that have been hidden for years.

Forgetting also illustrates the imperfection of memory. A person may forget because the brain has laid new memory patterns on top of old or, as in the case of old age, brain cells start to die off until a thought disappears.

An extraordinary memory

The most famous case of someone who could not forget was a patient of Soviet psychologist Aleksandr Luria—a young man known as S.— during the 1920s. A Moscow journalist, S. visited Luria to have his memory tested. Much to the doctor's surprise, S.'s memory appeared to have no limits. Detailed instructions, long lists, random numbers and words could be repeated without effort. Over a thirty-year period, Luria kept testing this amazing mnemonist, or person with a prodigious memory. He learned that S. memorized information like he was filming a motion picture; he could actually see pictures of everything—letters, words, etc.—in his head. And since he could not forget anything, S.'s mind could not focus and he constantly went off on tangents. As a consequence, S. could not hold down a job for long and he eventually spent his life doing memory performances.

Memory investigation abounds with fascinating anecdotes like the case of S. Researchers look for clues to the memory code in stories of people with ordinary to very low intelligence who have phenomenal memories, or others who have forgotten everything for many years. But just as baffling is the nature of even unexceptional memory. As the key to individual identity, it remains a vital subject of research.

3

Left Brain/
Right Brain

THE HUMAN BRAIN is virtually split in two. That fact has been known to brain researchers since the first brains were examined and observed. Huge cerebral bulges sit next to each other inside the skull, almost mirror images of each other, consisting of almost two-thirds of the total brain mass. The question that has begged scientific attention, however, is why? Why would the human brain have two sides? The puzzle of the left and right cerebral hemispheres has intrigued those who study human behavior, for they have noticed that a human being has two ways of thinking: creatively and logically. It might just be possible that the two sides of the brain are responsible for different kinds of function.

The search for answers

The most direct way of figuring out how the brain worked was by looking at brains that didn't. By the nineteenth century, researchers were starting to investigate the relationship between brain dysfunction and physical deformity. Evidence was building from surgeries and autopsies on people whose brains were damaged from sickness and injury.

(Opposite page) Although there is constant interaction between the right and left brain, research suggests that the two hemispheres control very different functions. The right brain, for instance, governs creativity and artistic ability.

51

In 1834, a French physician by the name of Marc Dax started to gather evidence about the relationship between brain injury and speech impairment. He reported that in his observations, all of the people who had lost their ability to speak had the left sides of their brain damaged. His conclusion, according to professor Sally Springer and neuropsychologist Georg Deutsch in their book *Left Brain, Right Brain*, "aroused virtually no interest among those who heard it and was soon forgotten. Dax died the following year, unaware that he had anticipated one of the most exciting and active areas of scientific inquiry of the second half of the twentieth century."

Broca's area of the brain

Twenty-five years later, Pierre Paul Broca, a French surgeon, announced the results of his autopsies on speech-impaired people. In one startling case, Broca told of a patient whose total ability to speak was limited to the words "tan, tan." At a gathering of scientists in Paris, he produced the brain of his patient after Tan Tan's death, revealing an egg-sized injury in the left hemisphere. His conclusion, which was confirmed by his other examinations of people with impaired speech, was that there was injury to a part of the left frontal lobe in all cases. Broca said: "It seems from all this that the faculty of articulate language is localized in the left hemisphere, or at least it depends chiefly upon that hemisphere." For his thoroughness and documentation, science rewarded Broca by naming that part of the brain associated with speech production after him.

Ironically, another physician examining a separate case discovered that even when speech was impaired with left brain damage, patients could still sing. Today, scientists know that musical

By studying the brains of speech-impaired patients, French surgeon Pierre Paul Broca identified a part of the brain vital to speech production.

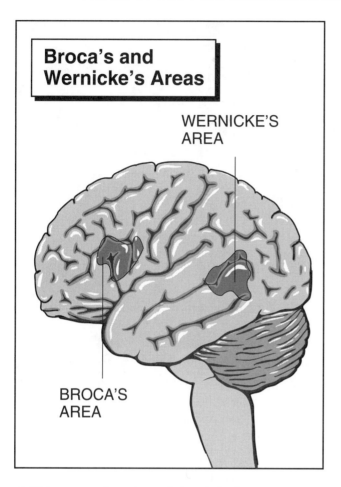

Broca's and Wernicke's Areas

WERNICKE'S AREA

BROCA'S AREA

abilities are a function of the right brain. But this finding still shows how complex are the functions of each hemisphere.

Broca's work established the study of research into brain localization, or the idea that there were separate functions in different parts of the brain. In the middle of the nineteenth century, many researchers who had heard of Broca's announcement began to accept the idea that functions like language were localized in the brain. This was confirmed by further evidence from neurologists such as Carl Wernicke, who also observed those with speech dysfunction in the 1870s. Like Broca, Wernicke also achieved immortality by

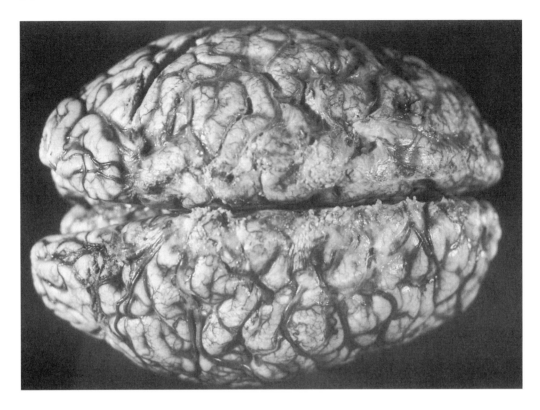

A photograph of the top of the brain shows its right and left hemispheres. While visual mirror images of one another, the two sides function quite differently.

having a language part of the brain named "Wernicke's area."

Further observations over the next century supported evidence that certain functions of the brain were located in specific areas. The greatest support for this conclusion resulted from a daring surgical technique developed in the 1940s. This technique allowed surgeons to literally split the brain in two.

Splitting the brain

The two cerebral hemispheres of the brain are connected by a bridge of nerve fibers called the corpus callosum. For a long time, the function of this fibrous bridge was puzzling. Neurologists and surgeons believed that it was the way that the two hemispheres communicated with each other. They pondered the question: What would happen if these millions of nerve fibers were cut? Would the two sides of the brain work independently or would one side take over for the other?

A revolutionary procedure

A revolutionary surgical operation designed to help sufferers of severe epilepsy would provide an answer. For those with the severe and incurable type of this disease, the explosion of nerve impulses that traveled from one hemisphere to the other was previously fatal if not responsive to medication. A courageous procedure developed in the 1940s by neurosurgeon William Van Wagenen severed the corpus callosum, thus preventing the seizures from crossing over and damaging both hemispheres. At least that was the theory. Multitudes of brain cells could be saved if the epileptic explosions were limited to just one hemisphere.

Van Wagenen's surgery was disappointing, however. As Sally Springer and Georg Deutsch point out, "Success in relieving seizures seemed to vary greatly from patient to patient." The outcome was unpredictable. The only consistent outcome was this: The patients who received this procedure did not suffer any apparent ill side effects from the brain splitting. Their personalities were the same; they could handle the same intellectual activities. For all practical purposes, they appeared normal. Those who interviewed these special "split brain patients," as they came to be called, reported that they did not notice anything unusual.

Unusual changes had taken place, though. It may not have been apparent at first; indeed, Van Wagenen discontinued his procedure based on the uneven results. But over a twenty-year period, scientists would realize that subtle changes in brain behavior had, in fact, taken place when the human brain was split. Starting in the fifties, Roger Sperry, a chief researcher at the University of Chicago and later at the California Institute of Technology, would pioneer this investigation along with two primary assistants. So important was this research that it not only provided evidence of the different functions of each cerebral hemisphere but also earned Sperry the 1981 Nobel Prize in medicine and physiology.

The split brain research

Sperry's first stage was with experiments on animals. With the assistance of a graduate student, Ronald Myers, he began studying cats. The optic nerves of the cats were severed and reattached so that the left brain's nerves were connected to the left eye and vice versa, preventing the left eye from communicating with the right side of the brain. Then the corpus callosum was severed, splitting the brain in half.

Pictures of a circle and square were shown to the cats. One eye was covered and the other was open. The cats had been taught how to tell the difference between the circle and square through rewards of food. Although the cats recognized the difference with each open eye, they forgot the difference when next given the same choice with the other eye.

From this and similar experiments, Sperry and Myers concluded that the two cerebral hemispheres functioned independently. In the case above, for instance, cats with unsevered brains would have had hemispheres that could have communicated with each other, hence they would not have forgotten the circle or square. The work of Sperry and associates became known as the "split brain studies."

Based on these studies, surgeons Philip Vogel and Joseph Bogen decided to revive the brain-

Roger Sperry won the 1981 Nobel Prize in medicine and physiology for his split brain research.

splitting operation on humans. Vogel and Bogen "reasoned that some of the earlier work with human patients had failed because the disconnection between the cerebral hemispheres was not complete," say Springer and Deutsch. Their revival was successful, and it set the stage for Sperry's next series of experiments on humans in the sixties.

Citing his experiments with cats, Sperry knew that split brains changed behavior. Ordinary behavior may remain the same, but certain types of behavior changed radically. To prove this, he created various subtle tests involving touch and sight that he could use on human patients. The tests—created with another assistant, Michael Gazzaniga—were designed to limit the data that could be communicated to one side or the other of the surgically altered brains.

Examining split brain patients

A forty-eight-year-old man Sperry and Gazzaniga called W. J. was their first test subject. W. J. had epilepsy and had elected to undergo the split brain surgery. The two scientists began analyzing W. J.'s vision after he submitted to the operation. A written message was flashed to the subject's left eye. The right hemisphere of the brain controls the left eye. W. J. had no response to the message. Sperry and Gazzaniga concluded that the right brain had little to do with language: W. J. could not understand the instruction and hence could not react to it. Another test requested that W. J. arrange colored blocks into a specific design. This was an easy task for the left hand, controlled by the right hemisphere, but the right hand, controlled by its opposite brain half, found the job a lot more difficult. Even though W. J. had already seen his left hand perform the task, his right hand could not. Did this mean that the right hemisphere was more specialized for constructing things that it could see? Sperry and Gazzaniga thought so. Says Gazzaniga: "The claim that we based on those findings was that the left hemisphere is dominant for language processes and the right hemisphere is dominant for visual-construction tasks." The patient could not identify any object put in the left hand, if blindfolded. The right brain may recognize the object, but it could not put the identification into speech.

The experiments were repeated over and over, with many variations, to make sure they were accurate. In each trial, the answers were the same. Neither side of the brain was aware of the activities of its opposite. At the extreme, these special tests yielded some unusual differences.

Differences between the hemispheres

Clearly, the right hemisphere did not possess the language and analytical skills of the left brain. On the other hand, it was not helpless. Sperry discovered that it did have certain crossover abilities. A few of the patients recognized words that were picked up by the right brain, whether flashed or spoken. Hearing is an activity that can be handled by either side of the brain. The one difference with the right brain is that objects can be recognized by description, but not by name. Other testing showed that the right brain could do simple addition and reasoning, skills that are more left-brain oriented. This led the researchers to believe that it might be possible for skills to be learned by both sides of the brain.

Through tests like this and others on split brain patients, and on subjects with no known physical disorders, the unique differences between the right and left hemispheres were demonstrated. They were remarkably independent. One test asked the patients to stare ahead while the letters "HE" were flashed to the left and "ART" were flashed to the right, spelling "HEART." When the patient was asked to name what he saw, he replied "ART." If the word "HEART" was presented to the patient, divided on two cards into "HE" and "ART," and the patient was requested to *point* to the word with the left hand, the word pointed to was "HE." Each hemisphere responded differently to the same experience. From this and similar experiments, Sperry concluded that the left hemisphere is responsible for speech while the right brain handles physical movement. Both sides of the brain could pick up sensory data, but only the left side could reply with a spoken answer.

Distinct functions

The fact that both sides of the brain seem to operate independently and have distinct functions has led to the speculation that maybe a human being has two separate personalities. Indeed, Sperry's associate Gazzaniga believed that not only did each half have its own way of looking at things, but that each might at times be at odds with each other—literally, that the left hand doesn't know what the right hand is doing. In one case, Gazzaniga tested both hemispheres of the brain of a young man with the same questions. The response was different for both sides, especially on days when the man was tense and anxious. The scientist concluded that anxiety perhaps is a by-product of hemispheric warring.

In the words of *Three-Pound Universe* authors Dick Teresi and Judith Hooper: "Occasionally the two hemispheres would be at odds, and a patient would find her left hand unbuttoning her blouse as quickly as the right hand could button it." In another case, Gazzaniga showed two sets of pictures to both sides of the brain. When the right side could not explain what it had just seen because of its poorer language abilities, the left side

Writing is an example of left brain activity. In Western society, the left brain is considered the dominant hemisphere.

took over with its higher language skills. Where speech or language is required, the superior left brain will take over to rationalize for the right.

Because the skills of the left brain are valued more highly than the right in Western society, the left brain has come to be called the dominant hemisphere. (It is also slightly larger than the right.) It is responsible, as shown from clinical studies, for qualities that are prized in our culture: concrete and rational thinking, logic, speech and writing, goal orientation. In advanced, industrial societies, these traits—essential to communication, math, and logic—are necessary. Cultures that place a greater emphasis on mysticism and art are generally right-brain thinkers. With all the emphasis placed on left-brain thinking, the right brain should not be downplayed. The left brain must do things logically and step by step. The right brain can grasp the big picture quickly and spontaneously.

Constant interaction

There is a constant interaction between the skills of the left brain and the right in everyday life. From research on the brain's workings, science has found that human beings have two different styles of thinking: the emotional, artistic, and intuitive (right brain) and the linear, analytic, and verbal (left brain). Most people lean to one side or the other in the way they handle problems and events. Their preference is influenced by family, heredity, and society. Early in life, people develop a preference for being left-brained or right-brained. Their skills come from their preferred hemisphere; their failings arise out of their less dominant side. That explains why someone may be good at math, but a lousy dancer.

In daily activities, a person uses the right hemisphere when they are listening to a music concert or painting the house. The left hemisphere is used when they are talking to a friend or figuring out their income tax. From moment to moment, the average person shifts back and forth between the two hemispheres, depending on the task that he or she is doing. Individuals usually do not change their preference throughout their lifetimes, although it is possible to develop the abilities of the less dominant hemisphere. A well-rounded person uses both sides of the brain equally well.

Because all testing of the two hemispheres of the brain had been done on patients who had physical disorders and had undergone radical surgery, not on normal, functioning human beings, some scientists argued that it was only because of the brain damage that the left and right hemispheres demonstrated such specialized functioning.

But later research in the sixties and seventies verified that normal, non–split brain people have the same right brain/left brain abilities as those who have had the operation. Such observations as eye movements, vision tests, and EEG examinations (measuring brain waves from each hemisphere) have been used to confirm the results.

Beyond the functional

There are differences between the hemispheres that go beyond the functional. An examination of the hemispheres themselves, for instance, reveals a unique physical difference. Because they develop at different rates, there is a minute variation in color. The right brain has more white matter, an insulation called myelin, which allows signals from nerve cells to be processed quickly. The left brain, which appears gray, does not have this same kind of insulation. The skills of the right brain developed earlier than those of the left, as they were the ones most concerned with survival. In a crisis, the insulated cells of the right brain could process the big picture in an instant, giving a person a gut feeling or hunch. A person might be dead before the left brain got around to logically figuring out what was wrong. The right brain was invaluable to the cave dweller. The left brain is critical to modern humans.

In short, the left brain is goal-oriented, rational, concrete, verbal, sequential, explicit, linear, and analytical. The right brain is physical, artistic, visual, playful, nonverbal, emotional, spontaneous. Walking around the block is a right-brain activity; taking an intelligence test comes from the left brain. Technical writing requiring logic is left-brain; creative writing involving improvisation is right-brain. The left brain plans the day, keeps life organized, and works on a time schedule. The right brain governs physical movement and imagination.

The ultimate mystery of the brain's two hemispheres may never be known. What is generally concluded by science is that the division of brain functions into the two sides is a relatively recent evolutionary phenomenon. Right about the time that humankind started advancing beyond pure survival and developed early writing and art, the brain started subdividing responsibilities. The qualities that make us distinctively human and civilized began growing. As humankind started using more and more intelligence, evolution made the brain less redundant. There was no need to have two hemispheres absolutely identical in function. The needs and problems of human beings were too complicated to have that kind of brain state. Hence, nature devised two separate ways of handling problems; both play vital roles.

"Nearly all discoveries in every field appear to involve a sudden right-brain inspiration," says Ronald Bailey. "Then the left-brain intellect laboriously works out the details of this hunch, step by step."

Interaction despite this specialization is constant, in both conscious daily activities and humans' surprisingly active periods of sleep.

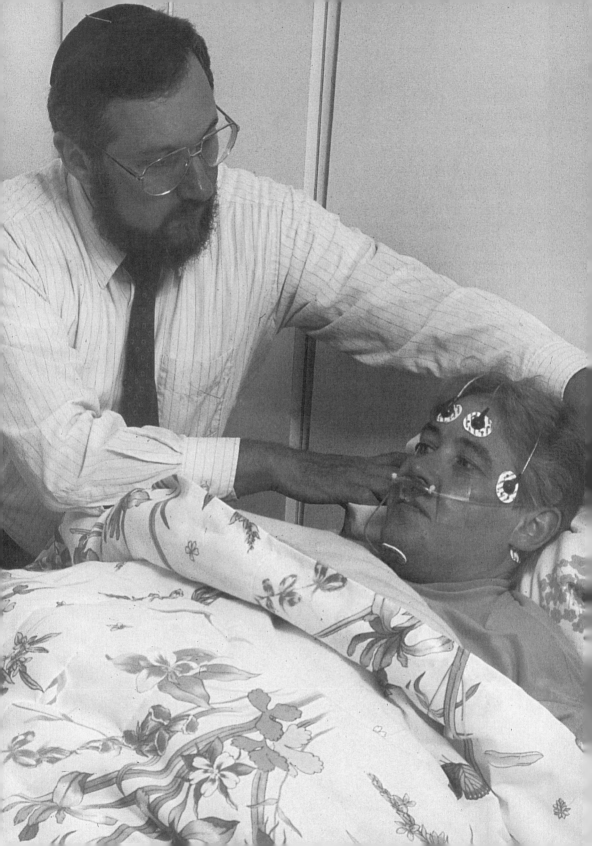

4

Sleeping and Dreaming

EVERY DAY, THE human brain takes us on a fantastic journey from alertness and concentration to deep, blissful sleep, with momentary stops off at daydreaming and meditation. It's a journey on which the average person spends twenty years of his or her lifetime, and it is one of the most baffling tours known to neuroscience. Ancient peoples saw sleep in many ways: as a metaphor for death, as a venture to a foreign land. Modern humans embrace sleep as a welcome escape from hectic daily life. Science has still another view of this interesting behavior. From a mix of research, much done in sleep labs around the world, scientists have watched the way the brain alters the stages of consciousness from concentration to slumber. Little by little, the pieces of the puzzle are starting to come together: what the ancients saw as a mystical experience, modern experts now see as electrochemical activity in the brain cells.

Most people take being awake for granted. It dominates the daytime hours and is the arena in which attention is most focused. It is a level of consciousness, and in this level the average person is alert, stimulated, and aware of what is go-

(Opposite page) By monitoring brain activity during sleep, scientists hope to uncover the mysteries of sleep.

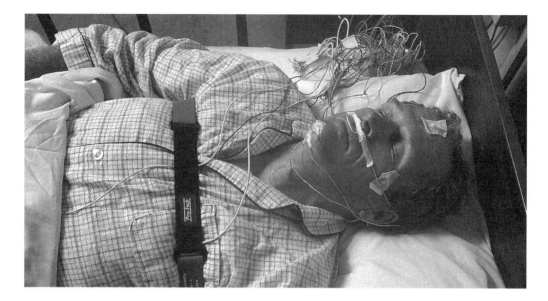

The EEG, or electroencephalograph, is attached to a subject through wires pasted to the scalp.

ing on. The other main state of consciousness, sleeping, is, it turns out, not the simple absence of activity it appears to be.

Measuring consciousness

It's relatively easy to tell when one is sleeping and one is awake. From a scientific point of view, however, only since the invention of the electroencephalograph, or EEG, has neuroscience known how the brain changes internally during this process. The most productive research has come from so-called sleep laboratories, where volunteers are attached to EEG machines that record their brain wave activity while they sleep. (Cameras also film the volunteers as a record of their habits and movements.)

Here's how the EEG works. The brain's electrochemical makeup shifts the types of waves that are traveling through its circuits, corresponding to the body shifts from wakefulness to sleep and everything in between. Attached to a subject through wires pasted to the scalp, the EEG machine picks up these changes in electrical voltage, and it's possible to graph these fluctuations as "brain waves." An intense state of alertness produces beta waves, fourteen to thirty cycles per second. More relaxed consciousness shifts into alpha waves, eight to thirteen cycles per second. Deep sleep slows down the wave cycles to fewer than 3.5 per second. The state of sleep in which dreaming occurs resembles a quick-paced beta.

The circadian rhythms, the twenty-four-hour daily cycles that influence both the brain and the body, are equally important. Following the rhythm of the earth's day, the average human being follows these cycles whether they are aware of them or not. In special experiments, volunteers who have lived in caves without clocks or awareness of day or night still have kept close to a twenty-four-hour cycle. Studies on this subject were carried out in the sixties in a German underground bunker and caves far below the surface in France. Much to the surprise of scientists, it was discovered that the human body will naturally shift to a twenty-four- or twenty-five-hour day, no matter what schedule it is put on.

Within these daily cycles are smaller cycles of ninety minutes apiece. These smaller sequences have become known as biorhythms and affect just about everything happening in the body. Brain activity peaks and wanes within these cycles, its nerve cells alternating from frenzied activity to relative calm. The times a day a person feels energetic, hungry, or any one of forty types of activity, can be traced to biorhythms. Mental alertness alternates with daydreaming. Even sleep is not immune from these cycles: The most intense dreams happen in the peaks of these cycles.

The biological clock

The body's biological clock is regulated from a small, pine cone–shaped brain part called the pineal gland, located at the top of the brainstem. The timekeeper of the body, the pineal picks up clues about light and dark from nerve communications from the eyes and matches that with the outside cycle of day and night. Once it's set in motion, it can keep fairly accurate time, allowing a person to function on a cycle of twenty-four or sometimes twenty-five hours. The pineal gland also has other functions: helping to initiate puberty, regulate menstruation, and produce the chemical serotonin, associated with sleep.

How the brain makes up its mind

The pineal gland is not an abrupt on/off switch. Just because it reacts to changes in the day and night cycles does not mean that it starts everyone sleeping when the sun goes down. Another part of

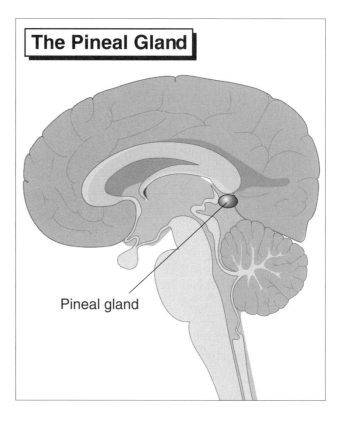

The Pineal Gland

Pineal gland

the brain actually has the job of switching awareness on and off, working with the pineal. Called the reticular activating system, or RAS, it is a small, dense cluster of nerve cells contained in the brainstem. Like a watchguard over information and awareness, it reacts to data coming from the senses, as well as memory, emotions, and thought. The brain is then alerted, and as the millions of messages hitting the brain compete for attention, the RAS separates them out, picks out the ones that are most important, and lets those few into areas above the brainstem.

It is on these messages that a person concentrates, allowing him or her to focus on the odd or important in a sea of bombarding information. Without this ability of the RAS, a person would never be able to concentrate. Nor would there be any brain trigger for danger or its threat. A mother's ability to identify the cry of her child in a crowded shopping mall is the work of the RAS. RAS nerve cell axons, the single fiber that transmits nerve impulses from a cell, are short, which means that communications can be zapped quickly from cell to cell. If a message comes in that requires attention in the cortex, it can send out an alert that can start the brain thinking.

Deprived of sensory stimulation

The brain seems to work best through this immersion in sensory excitement. A person denied this stimulation may become disorganized. A continuous bombardment of stimulation would be nerve-racking, and the brain compensates for this by switching back and forth between alpha and beta brain rhythms throughout the day. But the total absence of stimulation can be just as damaging as its opposite. In one famous Canadian experiment at McGill University in Montreal, subjects were blindfolded, their hands padded, and their ears and eyes covered. Robbed of all sensory stimulation, some of the volunteers quit in the middle of the experiment, while those who stayed on started hallucinating. A disabled RAS, in fact, one which has been damaged, will put a person in a coma.

The world of sleep

It was once thought that sleep was the time when the brain turned itself off. After all, if the body was resting, some reasoned, wouldn't the brain be resting also? The mystery of sleep became the subject of myths, folklore, and nursery rhymes. Science didn't take the subject of sleep seriously until the twentieth century. Until the invention of the technology that monitored brain waves, there were few clues as to what sleep was and why. When science finally started its surge of sleep research, what it discovered was amazing. "[There was] clear evidence that human dreaming is tied to a brain process of broad biological significance," says Harvard professor J. Allan Hobson in his book *The Dreaming Brain*. Far from being totally constant, sleep was a series of several brain states, as different as black and white.

The importance of sleep

The first trademark of sleep is that the breathing and heart rate slow down. The blood pressure drops. The muscles slacken. Organized thinking may break down into random thoughts. The mind drifts between wakefulness and fragile slumber. This is Stage 1 sleep, in which brain waves are on an irregular and low voltage. People may not even be aware that they are about to go to sleep. In the brain, the body's biological clock, the pineal gland, releases a hormone, melatonin, which influences the process that produces serotonin, the chemical transmitter related to sleep.

Sensory input to the reticular activating system is slowed down. All the electrical activity darting through the cerebral cortex diminishes until it dips below the point necessary to maintain wakefulness. The eyes can no longer stay open. The body wants to go to sleep.

In only a matter of minutes, drifting even further, one enters Stage 2. The eyes begin to roll from side to side. The brain shuts off what the eyes record so that, even if the eyes are opened, they wouldn't "see" anything. Only the brightest of lights will stimulate them. A small noise will still bring someone back to consciousness. Patterns of brain activity on the EEG become more irregular, marked by peaks and valleys. By Stage 3, the body relaxes even further; the major body functions drop even further, including temperature. The brain waves are large and slow, more even. The rolling of the eyes shifts from irregular to almost straight. A loud noise would be the only

In sleep laboratories, scientists record and study brain waves that reflect different states of consciousness.

sound that could awaken someone, as the sleeper is about to enter the deepest part of sleep.

Twenty minutes later, the sleeper enters Stage 4, so-called deep sleep. This is the time in which a sleeper may start talking or sleepwalking. Only the loudest of noises will bring someone out of deep sleep. The EEG charts show long, slow delta wave rhythms. This continues for another twenty minutes. At this point, a very interesting phenomenon occurs.

The cycle begins again—but this time it runs backwards. This is verified by the patterns the EEG pens are making on the graph. For the next thirty minutes, Stage 4 drifts into Stage 3, Stage 3 moves into Stage 2, and then, to Stage 1. Looking only at the EEG, it might appear that this person was awake. But the brain waves are actually signaling something else. This type of Stage 1 is radically different from the type experienced at the beginning of sleep. Dreaming is about to start up.

REM

This is the REM period. REM, for rapid eye movement, is the first of two major brain wave patterns that dominate sleep. The brain shifts into REM about every ninety minutes. During REM, a sudden transformation overtakes the body. The cerebral cortex is bombarded by signals from noradrenalin cells in the brainstem. Breathing becomes irregular. The eyes start darting from side to side. The sleeper tosses and turns. Dreams become more intense. The sleeper is as far removed from waking as he will ever be in his sleep.

REM sleep was virtually unheard of until it was discovered at the University of Chicago in the early 1950s. Nathaniel Kleitman, the director of the sleep laboratory, noticed that the eyes of both infants and adults zigzagged rapidly, even while the lids were closed. The moment this happened, EEG machines registered a radical change in brain wave patterns. Those sleepers who were awakened while in REM sleep consistently said that they had been dreaming. The more rapidly the eyes flickered, the more vivid were the subjects' dreams.

Between REM cycles, NREM, or the non-REM cycle, occurs. In NREM, breathing, body temperature, and heartbeat slow down and sleep is relatively peaceful. The movements of the eye are equally peaceful and rolling.

The first period of REM sleep is brief, approximately ten minutes long, but each REM period after that will get progressively longer until the slow-wave periods of deep tranquil NREM sleep gradually evaporate. The last hour of sleep may be almost entirely composed of eye-fluttering REM. The reticular activating system changes the brain wave patterns in the cortex and the sleeper wakes up.

The importance of sleeping and dreaming

Everyone needs sleep. It is the "shut-down" period in which the body repairs itself and the brain can organize daily events. Researchers have speculated that REM sleep is the time in which the brain sorts out the many stimuli that have bombarded it. People who have been deprived of sleep for long periods of time in special experiments become disoriented and suffer from hallucinations. The brain apparently needs a certain amount of dreaming as well as sleeping. Professor J. Allan Hobson says: "Dreaming . . . provides us with a remarkable mirror of our inner selves." People who have been cheated out of dreams one night make up for it the night after until the brain reaches the satisfaction point it needs. Those who were awakened at the point of dreaming and deprived of REM sleep also experienced major changes in personality, such as going from quiet to erratic.

Exactly how much sleep each person needs varies. Some people can get by on only one or two hours. Others, including infants and senior citizens, may need much more sleep, up to sixteen hours a day for infants. The required amount of sleep gradually diminishes into early adulthood, where sleep length is established. The average length of sleep for adults is seven or eight hours. Infants may routinely sleep fourteen hours a day, but most of infant sleep is REM sleep. The length of deep sleep starts to decline after middle age.

Sleep requirements also differ according to stress and personality. The more exertion or anxiety someone has been through, the greater the need for sleep. Not only must the body recuperate, but the brain needs more time, through REM, to file the experiences of the day. Personality, too, plays a part in the length of sleep. Several research studies have theorized that the longer one sleeps, especially beyond one's physical and mental requirements, the greater the likelihood that one is trying to escape from reality. Short sleepers, one researcher found, were more optimistic about facing the day. Longer sleepers would prefer the shelter of sleep than the daily anxiety. In fact, sleep cycles themselves have been found to be the causes of such emotional illnesses as depression. Richard Restak writes in *The Brain* that "studies at the National Institute of Mental Health and elsewhere suggest that at least some of the symptoms of depression and mania may be due to changes . . . [in] sleep."

The meaning of dreams

Dream detectives throughout the centuries have viewed dreams as having some great significance. Ancient prophets interpreted them as crystal balls into the future. Others saw them as guides to understanding human nature. Some tribal cultures thought of dreams as a separate parallel world, as real as their own. Poets wrote about them. Scientists used them to solve complex questions. Guides to interpreting the symbolism of dreams sprang up and have been around since ancient Egypt.

Everyone knows what a dream is, although few people know how to define one. A dream is a remembered experience. No one can talk about a dream while it is occurring; people always refer to dreams in the past tense. A person may think that they are observing a dream and someone may, in fact, awaken in the middle of a dream. But a dream is only a dream after a person awakens and identifies it as one. The one exception is the so-called lucid dreamer.

First identified by Stanford sleep researcher Stephen LaBerge in the late 1970s, lucid dreamers are those who are actually aware that they're dreaming. In specialized sleep lab experiments, LaBerge showed that one person in ten had this ability and could be trained through preselected eye movement codes to communicate to the outside world that they were in REM.

Dream recall

Each night, sleepers experience four or five dream periods. An eight-hour sleep can yield more than a dozen dreams. REM dreams are the most vivid, but dreams can happen in other sleep stages. Much of the time, the dreams are not remembered. Only three people out of ten can remember any dream. For some reason not precisely known to science, dreams are best recalled by accident. People can recall even tiny details in dreams if accidentally awakened, yet after the dream period is finished, their memory for specifics is reduced. Some dreams are kept in memory since childhood; others are fragments which will not survive the night.

Unconscious desires

Psychologists also believe that one of the reasons dreams escape the memory is that they deal with unconscious desires. So shocking or emotional are these dreams that their memory is repressed. Those dreamers who are more sensitive to their feelings have better recall. Stories of dreamers who have awakened and jotted down memories from their dreams are misleading. Often, the brain disguises this recall: What was written down in the heat of a dream is confusing the next day. A few authors even believe that it is possible to ask the brain to work on a problem during the night, sleep on it, let the brain go into a REM state, and wake up the next day with the answer to that problem. Some of the lucid dreamers think they can do just that.

Dreams may seem like everyday life. In fact, the characters and locations in dreams are more likely to be commonplace than not. This has been verified by the large numbers of dreams that have been collected scientifically over the last hundred years. Dreams, researchers found, have patterns. Author Ronald Bailey says: "One of the strangest results of the recent dream research is the discovery of the universality of dreaming." Sexual activity is quite common. Violence is less frequent. Dreams dealing with basic emotions like fear and anger are most prevalent. More dreams have settings in a house than on a road. Most dreams include the dreamer, either passively or actively.

The difference between dreams and the waking world, certainly, is that logic is suspended in dreams. Dreams may move from one place to another in an instant. Time has no meaning in dreams. Characters in dreams may do strange things or even be strangers. Researchers have found that there is a relationship between a previous day's events and a night's dreaming. Early dreams are affected by the least expected events, the insignificant and mundane. Dreams towards the end of sleep will reach deep in the brain's memory for substance. That is why dreams at this time seem like recollections from childhood.

Sigmund Freud

Until the end of the nineteenth century, science didn't take the study of dreams that seriously. Although other dream analyzers may have developed guides to understanding the symbols of dreams with little scientific basis, experts dismissed most of it as quackery. Not until Sigmund Freud, the founder of psychoanalysis, came on the scene were dreams accorded respect as a scientific subject. Working with patients called hysterics, subjects who had physical problems but no physical cause, Freud began probing their minds as they discussed their dreams. His conclusions were published in his famous book *The Interpretation of Dreams*, written in 1900.

Freud believed there was a relationship between dreams and the unconscious. He developed a theory that much of what cannot be explained about human behavior is caused by "repressed emotions." Repressed emotions are feelings and desires that a person cannot consciously accept, but which are released at night in dreams. According to authors Judith Hooper and Dick Teresi, "Freud said that in our dreams we visit a psychic Jurassic age, prehistoric, irrational, garbled, full of monsters." Understanding dreams can be a key to understanding the reasons why people have emotional problems. Hence, by look-

ing for the meaning in dreams, Freud felt he could reveal the secrets of the unconscious.

In the view of neurologists, who dominate contemporary dream theory, dreams simply have a physiological basis. Specifically, the pons of the brainstem secretes a chemical called acetylcholine that alerts the dormant cortex and activates dreaming. Another part of the brainstem, the locus coeruleus, produces another chemical, noradrenalin, which starts REM sleep. The reason dreams seem so bizarre is that the cortex is struggling to organize the nerve signals from the lower brain. In the search to link together all the contradictory data it has received, the brain may give the dreamer distorted or fantastic images. Experts also believe that the right brain may be more responsible for dreaming, since emotional functions are controlled there and vivid dreaming is lost to those with right-brain damage.

Although Freud was very influential in the field of psychology, many of his ideas are not popular today. Instead of viewing dreams as products of the unconscious, many neuroresearchers see them as the random firing of neurons in the nervous system. The brain needs a way to "unlearn" everything that it has been forced to absorb. REM sleep allows the brain to unravel the neural nets that have been connecting throughout the day.

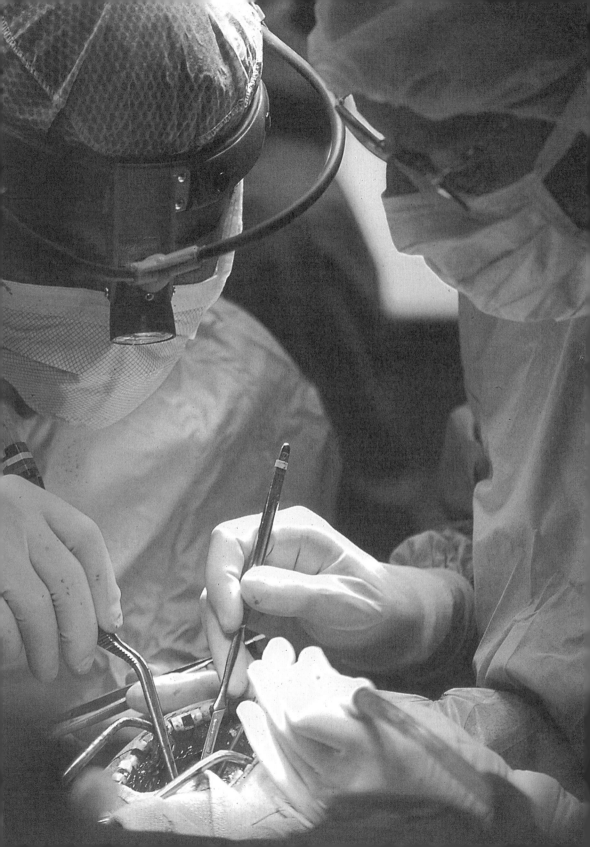

5

Brain Diseases and Disorders

FOR ALL ITS abilities and potential, the human brain is amazingly vulnerable. Even though it is protected by a sturdy skull and the insulation of the blood-brain barrier, special membranes that filter chemical activity between the bloodstream and central nervous system, its health can be affected by any number of disorders and ailments. Some of these malfunctions are manifested at childbirth—such as mental retardation associated with Down's syndrome—and may last a lifetime. The onset of others may not occur until late middle age, such as Alzheimer's disease, which renders its victim a helpless mental cripple. A few disorders, including senile dementia, may affect the brains of relatively many persons. At least one, Huntington's chorea, began ravaging succeeding generations of one small English village, but has now spread throughout the world. After millions of years of evolution, the brain is still susceptible to sickness.

Much of the work done with brain chemistry has focused on ailments of the brain. Computer-based brain scanners can both locate and detect the growth of tumors and the effects of strokes, epilepsy, and Huntington's chorea. Advances in

(Opposite page) The development of neuroscience has had a profound effect on the treatment of disorders and diseases of the brain.

pharmaceutical research have discovered drugs that can neutralize, at least temporarily, the effects of Parkinson's disease and schizophrenia. Experiments have actually been done in which fetal animal brain tissue has been transplanted in the hopes of future success with human brain transplants. Ideas that have been the topic of science fiction may someday make the ailments of the brain a thing of the past.

Until that time, however, science must cope with medical problems that affect millions and cost billions in treatment and caregiving. As reporter Alicia Hills Moore says in *Fortune* magazine: "According to the Society for Neuroscience, located in Washington, D.C., fully one sixth of the U.S. population—48 million people—suffer from brain disorders. . . . The estimated annual cost of medical care for all these afflictions is at least $400 billion." From birth to death, the brain faces a threatening array of malfunctions.

Brain defects at birth

The most common inherited defects directly related to the brain include anencephaly, in which a baby is born without a brain—a condition that is always fatal—and hydrocephalus, in which cerebrospinal fluid is trapped, causing an enlarged head. Hydrocephalus, while treatable, can cause blindness, paralysis, and death unless the fluid is drained. Even with surgery, the prognosis for recovery is guarded, and complications like retardation and loss of muscle control can result.

Two other well-known conditions affect the growing fetal brain—cerebral palsy and Down's syndrome. Cerebral palsy is believed to have a number of causes, including when an infant's brain is deprived of vital oxygen and/or glucose. Other causes may include heredity, prematurity,

This photograph of a hydrocephalic baby shows the infant's enlarged head in which cerebrospinal fluid is trapped.

the degree of maternal prenatal care, and environmental toxins.

In cerebral palsy, defects in the brain—specifically those areas that govern motor activity like the motor cortex, basal ganglia, and cerebellum—as well as the nervous system result in a breakdown of muscular power. Motor movement is usually impaired, and seizures and speech disorders are common, as is mental deficiency. There are three types of the disorder: spastic (tense, clenched movement), athetoid (unwanted movement), and ataxic (clumsiness). An estimated seven thousand children born each year in the United States are afflicted with cerebral palsy.

Down's syndrome is the most common cause of congenital abnormality. Named after Langdon Down, the English physician who first noted it in 1866, the syndrome is found in roughly one-third of all seriously mentally retarded children in America. It is a genetic defect resulting from an extra chromosome in early development. One in one thousand births is affected; and the incidence increases with mothers who are over the age of forty. Down's syndrome infants are born with distinctive facial features, including a slant to the

The distinctive physical characteristics of Down's syndrome are apparent in this photograph of a young girl afflicted with the genetic disorder.

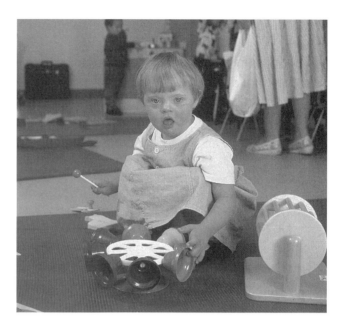

eyes, pug-shaped nose, and a large tongue. Defects of the heart and lungs are also apparent.

The seriousness of Down's symptoms varies widely. Only a minority of cases are serious enough to require institutionalization. Over half of the victims of Down's syndrome are classified as moderately retarded, with IQs of 30 to 50. Many Down's children can, with enlightened treatment, eventually lead a constructive and happy life.

Infections

Microorganisms—viruses, bacteria, fungi—can also attack the brain. They can reach the brain through a wound in the skull, an irritated ear, the nasal sinuses, via the bloodstream from some other part of the body, even traveling through a nerve, leaving infection and inflammation in their wake. Usually, the natural immune system of the body takes care of most of the infections, but some are serious enough to critically affect brain health.

Encephalitis and meningitis are the two main types of infections that affect the central nervous system. The first hits the brain directly; the second goes after the outer coverings of the brain, called the meninges. The encephalitis virus is usually carried by a mosquito or tick. It invades the brainstem, basal ganglia, and the cerebral cortex, injuring many nerve cells. No cure yet exists, although some symptoms—which include fever, vomiting, stiff neck and back, and more serious neuronal damage—may be relieved by medicine.

Meningitis afflicts the inner meningeal coverings of the brain: The meningitis bacteria plug the pathways of the inner coverings with pus, blocking fluids and, in turn, putting pressure on the brain. It is usually a complication of another infection and can eventually involve the brain's three meningeal membranes. Symptoms include fever, intracranial pressure, and muscle spasms—and can progress to delirium and stupor. The most common type is called viral meningitis and is mild enough to have a duration period of only two weeks. The more serious version is bacterial meningitis, whose symptoms can flare into coma. If left untreated, it can leave lasting brain damage. Unlike encephalitis, all types of meningitis can be cured totally—if they are caught in time. Generally, meningitis will not result in serious or permanent injury.

Rabies and polio

Other infections that can affect the brain include rabies and polio. The rabies virus moves through the nervous system until it reaches the brain—specifically the cerebellum, the hippocampus, and the medulla—where it destroys nerve cells, leaving behind small trace particles called Negri bodies, which are its trademark. The victim, once bitten by an infected animal, initially becomes irritable and nervous.

As the disease progresses, it can reach a furious stage and the patient may develop such an intense fear of water that he or she is unable to swallow saliva. This is called hydrophobia and manifests itself in violent spasms in the muscles and throat, combined with a feeling of terror. Untreated, the disease is generally fatal, but fortunately a vaccine developed from duck embryos is available, replacing an older and more painful treatment invented by Louis Pasteur. About twenty thousand people each year are vaccinated against rabies in the United States.

At one time polio produced a very real fear in the United States. Virtually unknown until 1916, an epidemic hit New York that year, killing some

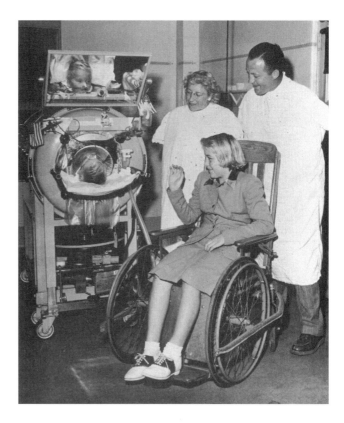

A young girl with polio visits another polio victim who can breathe only with the help of an iron lung. This crippling disease struck terror in the hearts of many until a vaccine was developed in the 1950s.

two thousand children. The disease caused the wasting of muscles and paralysis, sparked by an airborne virus that devoured motor neurons in the spinal cord. In severe cases that affected the muscles in the heart and lungs, victims often spent time in a tubelike machine called an iron lung. The machine produced a rhythmic pressure on the chest to help the patients breathe.

Author James Wynbrandt explains the difference between two competing polio vaccines. "The Salk vaccine, which is given by injection, is prepared by killing the virus with formalin. The dead virus cannot cause the disease, but it stimulates the production of antibodies that confer immunity. The Sabin vaccine, given by mouth, contains a [weakened] virus which can no longer cause disease symptoms, but stimulates the production of antibodies." Thanks to these vaccines—of which the Sabin vaccine is the most popular—a whole generation of Americans has reached adulthood without having to worry about polio.

Tumors

Tumors were first classified by the Greek physician Galen, who called them either benign or malignant, the Latin for good and evil, respectively. A benign tumor may grow slowly, whereas its counterpart, a malignant tumor, may spring up so quickly it can kill someone in months. The majority of brain tumors are cancerous. Malignant or cancerous tumors are haphazard growths of cells that do not match the cells around them. They grow more rapidly and eventually dominate their body area. However, even a benign tumor can create fatal pressure inside the cranium. An untreated tumor squeezes the brain, destroying brain cells, sometimes leading to death. The most common type is generated from the connective tissue of the brain, the neuroglia. Headaches, vision problems, vomiting, damage to specific brain functions, even psychotic behavior are all symptoms associated with growing brain tumors.

Brain tumors are most often removed surgically. The first successful brain surgery techniques were introduced a century ago when a brain tumor was successfully excised by William Keen in the United States in 1888. Treatment became much more sophisticated with the development of brain scanners in the twentieth century. Based generally on the principles of X-ray technology, but with the addition of advanced computers, scanners offered still-photo and moving videos of the structure and metabolic activity inside the head, pictures which could be helpful in diagnosing disease. CAT scans, which produced still pictures, were the forerunners of this technology and involved placing a patient's head inside a special X-ray ring where pictures could be taken from 360 degrees. CAT scans distinguished both the location and growth of tumors.

PET scans

PET scans are more sophisticated. A radioactive glucose substance is injected into a patient's bloodstream and a computer-based, three-dimensional X ray is performed. PET Scans observe the metabolizing of glucose in the brain and translate that activity into multicolor moving videos. In addition to helping science understand the workings of the brain—for instance, where thoughts originate—PET scans, as authors Judith Hooper and Dick Teresi say, "can pick out subtle tumors," because malignant tumors burn glucose faster than does healthy tissue.

The degree of a tumor's malignancy and its location in the brain will directly affect the success of its removal. If its cancer is spreading or the tumor is difficult to reach, the tumor may not be operable. If a tumor can be removed, then the surgeon who specializes in this practice, a neurosurgeon, will have to cut a flap in the skull to remove the diseased tissue. Because of the delicate nature of this type of surgery, it must be done very precisely and carefully as one slip of the scalpel could have devastating effects.

Strokes

Hippocrates called it "apoplexy." In modern times, it is referred to as a stroke. Strokes are the most common cause of serious physical disability in the United States and are the third largest cause of death behind heart attack and cancer. Almost half a million people, mostly over sixty, are struck down each year, half of those fatally. Also called "cerebrovascular accidents," strokes happen when the blood supply to the brain is blocked or, more frequently, cerebral blood vessels leak. The brain is deprived of oxygen and glucose, resulting in damage to nerve cells.

The CAT scanner is an advanced X-ray instrument that uses a computer to create a precise image on a screen. Here, an image of a patient's brain appears on the computer screen to the right.

Anthony Smith explains the terrible effects of strokes. "[I]t is injury to the most oxygen-demanding and unforgiving part of the body, the one least able to cope with insult. Damage to the brain can be dramatic in its effects upon the body as a whole. A normal human can become a hemiplegic, incapable of movement on the opposing side, unable [perhaps] to speak, unable to even prevent that half of the face from sagging wretchedly. And all because of a hiccup in the blood supply, a clot or hemorrhage whose effect elsewhere might not have even been noticed."

Three types of strokes

Strokes fall into three categories. When one of the brain's blood vessels bursts, it is called a cerebral hemorrhage. In this case, blood from the heart is pumped into the brain tissue, generating a blood clot that causes neural damage. The brain's blood vessels are among the weakest in the body, and defective vessel walls or high blood pressure can cause them to rupture. If the stroke is massive enough in the brain, it can rapidly cause unconsciousness and death.

The second type of stroke is called cerebral thrombosis and is caused by an obstruction in one of the brain's blood vessels. This type commonly afflicts middle-aged and elderly people. Once deprived of vital oxygen and glucose, brain cells die and the functions derived from that particular brain area are seriously affected. Dr. Arthur Ancowitz says: "Thrombotic strokes injure only a specific area of the brain supplied by a specific blood vessel and, in so doing, cause specific functional impairment." Stroke's third crippler has been named cerebral embolus. In this type of stroke, a fragment of clot substance travels through the bloodstream from the heart and gets lodged in a narrowed brain blood vessel. A potential crippler at any age, it is becoming increasingly rare due to anticlotting drugs.

A person undergoing a stroke experiences dizziness, slurred speech, and more often than not, temporary or permanent paralysis. Fortunately for stroke patients, medical science has leaped forward in stroke prevention and treatment. Specialized drugs now help to neutralize the conditions leading to embolic and hemorrhagic strokes by, for instance, helping to lower blood pressure. In patients who have suffered temporary strokelike symptoms, drugs can enlarge the affected blood vessels so as to avoid a more serious accident. And physicians have at their disposal revolutionary new tools: scanning devices for identifying strokes and microsurgery devices for treating blocked arteries.

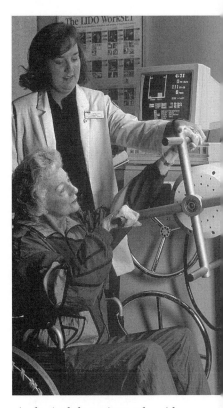

A physical therapist works with a patient recovering from a stroke. Strokes occur when blood supply to the brain is cut off.

Epilepsy

Richard Restack describes an epileptic seizure in *The Brain*: "One moment all is calm. Then, suddenly, everything comes apart. Chaos ensues, terror, horror. Some spectators turn away, others want to help but don't know how, still others stare transfixed. A fall; abrupt unconsciousness perhaps heralded by a scream; jerking, violent contraction of the body; more noises, more jerking, and then as suddenly as it began, the seizure is over." What seems like an eternity usually passes in less than a minute.

Once thought to be influenced by the moon or triggered through witchcraft, epilepsy is now known to be caused by abnormal electrical discharges of the brain. Epileptic seizures can be triggered by anything—stress, overwork, low blood sugar, deep breathing, drinking too much water, even just listening to the wrong musical notes. According to the World Health Organization, there are as many as forty million epileptics around the world.

Forms of epileptic convulsions vary. In the Jacksonian fit, a tremor traditionally begins in one area of the body—say, just a finger—and usually spreads to the face. The seizure is named after John Hughlings Jackson, a self-taught farmer's son who recorded his wife's convulsions.

All types of epilepsy are defined by the type of seizure. A petit mal seizure is a less severe version of the disorder. The victim's consciousness clouds briefly, so quickly that he or she may not be aware of the seizure. Expression may go blank. In fact, the only way that the petit mal can be detected is through an EEG reading. The most severe form of epileptic seizure is the grand mal. The victim loses consciousness immediately, falling to the ground. The body gyrates in exhausting spasms that alternate between stiffness and relaxation. The tongue may be bitten; there may even be foam at the mouth. As the neuron firing decreases, the attack slows down.

Three-quarters of all epileptic patients can lead close to normal lives due to improvements in antiepileptic drugs and diagnostic techniques. New brain scanning methods allow scientists to precisely track the location of epileptic attacks. In a process called intensive monitoring, specialized equipment is used to match videotapes of patients' seizures with EEG readings to record the path of the electrical discharges in the brain and the behavior they produce.

Degenerative diseases

Neurology's major degenerative diseases produce a variety of progressive brain-related symptoms and disabilities, from a gradual loss of skills to death. These diseases include Parkinson's disease, multiple sclerosis, Huntington's chorea, and Alzheimer's disease.

Older people between the ages of fifty and seventy-five are the main victims of Parkinson's. As many as half a million Americans may suffer from this trembling disease. Its effects may be slight at first, such as an uncontrollable trembling noticeable in small areas, but the disease can progress to other muscular parts of the body after many years. Handwriting becomes cramped and the voice quavers. The major joints lose their elasticity and mobility. It can also cause mental dementia. New hope in treating this disease came in 1976 with the development of a drug called L-dopa, which is a synthetic version of a brain chemical called dopamine.

L-dopa

L-dopa was developed after scientists discovered that Parkinson's caused certain cells in the brain to die off. These cells produce a substance called dopamine, which controls the motor nerves that keep our hands steady and move our facial muscles to make a smile. High doses of L-dopa reversed most of the symptoms of Parkinson's—at least, temporarily. Patients who had been shackled with shaking limbs and rigid muscles began to have more control over their own movements. Unfortunately, the results were not permanent. The effect would wear off and unwanted side effects would appear, including immobility and personality changes. It was all a lesson, as authors Judith Hooper and Dick Teresi said, "that the brain was not a simple machine that can be repaired by adding X grams of a single chemical."

Multiple sclerosis (MS), loosely translated as multiple scars in reference to the scars found on the brain's myelin sheaths, was unidentified in the American medical community until 1867. It is a disease that attacks the nerves of the spinal cord, brainstem, cerebral hemispheres, and the optic nerve—and young adults are the most likely victims. Its cause is unknown. Multiple sclerosis affects a part of the nerve cell called the myelin sheath, involved in signaling other neurons. A fatty, soft matter that insulates the nerve fibers, myelin breaks down under the disease. Scar tissue forms on the sheaths, interrupting the flow of nerve signals throughout the body. Symptoms may start with a temporary loss of vision leading to a decline of strength and coordination and, finally, death. Ironically, myelin can repair itself. Yet as Dr. Louis Rosner and Shelley Ross explain in their book *Multiple Sclerosis*, the only thing this means is "that MS is usually associated with many attacks . . . and recoveries." There is no known cure.

Huntington's chorea

Huntington's chorea is the most unusual of the degenerative diseases because all the mutations of this disorder originated from one family living in a small village in England four centuries ago. It was described by Dr. George Huntington in a paper he read before the Academy of Medicine in 1872. The disease, he said, was an ailment of the middle aged. Jerky movements erupted in the face and arms, leading to persistent degeneration that can turn a once normal, healthy person into a demented, confused cripple.

Medical historians have traced the disease in America to three male immigrants who settled in New York in 1630 and fathered children with a strange sickness. The majority of those who have HD in the United States today—some 25,000 confirmed and 125,000 at risk—inherited the disease from these three men. Huntington's involves a degeneration of the cerebrum and basal ganglia. Nerve cells that control movement and carry impulses are destroyed, leading to symptoms such as uncontrollable movements, compulsive clenching and unclenching, and forgetfulness. There is no known cure, although drugs relieve some of the movement problems. Brain scanning has become a way of predicting who might get the disease. A genetic test is now available that positively identifies those who carry the defect.

Alzheimer's disease

Over four million people in the United States suffer from Alzheimer's disease, making it the fourth leading cause of death in this country. Described first by Alois Alzheimer in 1909, it is part of an overall disorder called dementia, which is associated with forgetfulness, lack of recall, and, as the disease progresses, instability, paranoia, confusion, lack of body control, inability to perform simple tasks, and general helplessness. Alzheimer's and dementia are the main reasons for nursing home confinement for the elderly.

Until Alzheimer's discovery, senility was always thought to be an essential part of the aging process. Alzheimer changed all that, and proved that dementia was related to specific damage in the brain. Scientists still are not sure what causes Alzheimer's, and they have not ruled out slow viruses and environmental toxins. But what they do know is that filaments in the cerebral cortex and the hippocampus become twisted and tangled, and that the brain chemical neurotransmitter called acetylcholine, involved in memory, also appears to be affected. Much research still needs to be done, and scientists are currently studying abnormal proteins in the blood, the chemistry of the tangled filaments, and external influences on the brain.

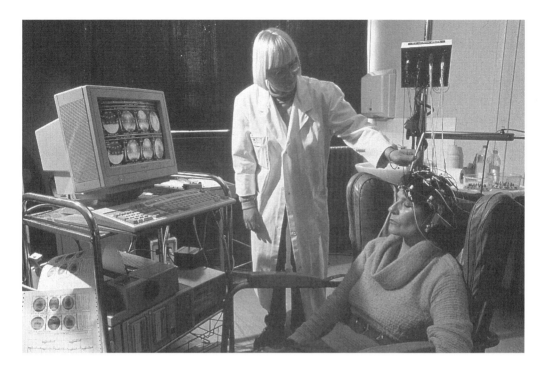

A medical researcher searching for clues about Alzheimer's disease examines the electrical activity of the brain as recorded by an EEG.

For centuries, emotionally unstable people were treated harshly. In the Middle Ages, they were burned at the stake or shackled in chains and confined to dank cells. Some believed the mentally ill were possessed by the devil or were incurable criminals.

In the nineteenth century, victims of mental illness were recognized as medical problems. Institutions and humane care, for the most part, replaced penal colonies and prisons, depending on the type of emotional condition. When Sigmund Freud introduced psychiatry to the world, periods of madness were blamed on unhappy childhoods and subconscious repression.

Only in the last four decades have scientists begun to understand that most mental illnesses—including schizophrenia and depression—are products of biochemistry in the brain, specifically neurotransmitters, substances which help send messages between nerve cells. When these messengers were no longer working, a person's moods and emotions could change.

Schizophrenia and depression

Schizophrenia was first recognized by a Swiss psychiatrist named Eugen Bleuler in 1911. After examining hundreds of patients, he identified four sets of symptoms that followed those with this split personality: indecision, obsessive withdrawal, illogical associations, and inappropriate emotions. As Richard Restak says: "the schizophrenic appears to live in a 'different reality' than the rest of us." Schizophrenia means "splitting of the brain" and schizophrenics seem afraid of the world, confused and lonely—with thought disorders and delusions. About 1 percent of the American population is a victim of this illness.

The turning point in the treatment of schizophrenia came in the 1950s with the discovery of a drug, chlorpromazine, which helped reduce the thought disorders of the disease, virtually eliminating the more extreme symptoms. Unfortunately, it took scientists another ten years to understand why this drug worked. Chlorpromazine reduced the amount of dopamine, a neurotransmitter produced by the brain, especially in those parts close to the limbic system, known to be pivotal in creating emotions. Drugs derived from chlorpromazine helped to soften some of the symptoms, although they didn't cure the disease. Scientists have also found that schizophrenic brains have basic cellular damage, a fact confirmed by high-resolution brain scans.

Depression is another mental disorder that scientists now understand is partially hereditary. Depression is a chronic disorder for which there may be no external cause. In studies done at the National Institute of Mental Health, researchers found that depression was linked to a deficiency of two vital neurotransmitters, norepinephrine and serotonin. Scientists have theorized that these neurotransmitters break down or aren't being released properly in the hypothalamus and limbic system, the brain's pleasure centers, causing mood changes. Antidepressants that increase the level of either or both of these neurotransmitters have proven effective in leveling out depression.

The brain has such a delicate chemical balance that even if only one chemical is off by 5 percent, as Ronald Kotulak says, it can "set in motion a chain reaction of chemical errors that result in a wide variety of mental problems, including aggression, alcoholism, drug abuse, and criminal violence." The day may not be far off when crime and mental illness can be eliminated by altering brain chemicals.

Predictions and cures

While many brain diseases and disorders are frightening in their bleak prognoses, the future does hold out new hope. Each month, groundbreaking developments, are discovered that may alter the future of brain ailments. For example, a new gene has been identified that could be the key to the cause of early Alzheimer's. This discovery may lead to a cure. Another new surgical technique could also show promise in treating both Alzheimer's and Parkinson's. Surgeons have burned selected nerve cells in brains of Parkinson's victims and have been able to halt all the trembling symptoms, bringing relief to many. In another technique, researchers have carried out experiments transplanting neurotransmitter-rich fetal brain matter in animals. These transplants could result in the same processes being performed on victims of Parkinson's and Alzheimer's.

Richard Restak effectively summarizes the importance of this research when he says: "If the brain is what makes us human, then disruptions and distortions in normal brain functioning can be expected to impair our humanity." The quality of human life is directly and intrinsically related to the health of the human brain.

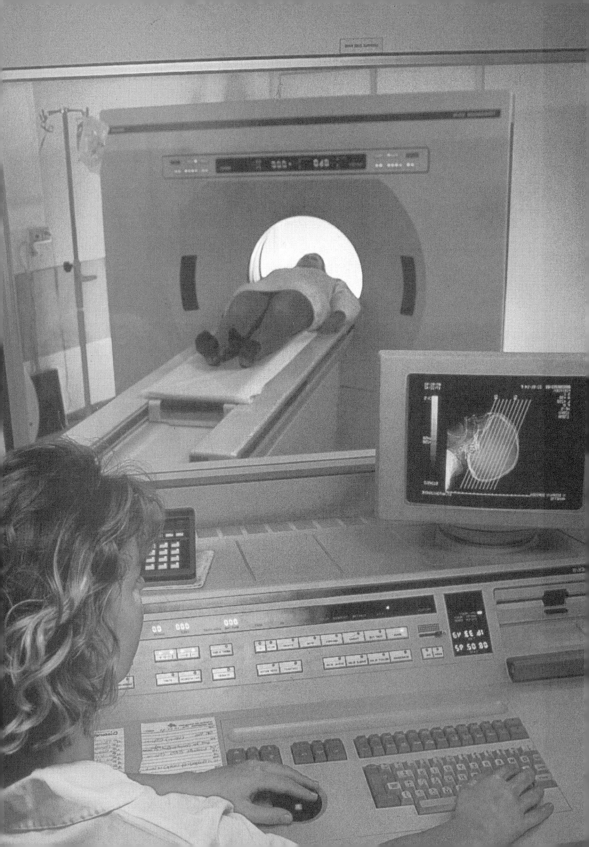

6

Windows to the Brain

IN A BOOK ENTITLED *Discovering the Brain*, published by the National Academy of Sciences, James Watson, the codiscoverer of DNA, makes the point that the brain "was the most complex thing that we have yet discovered in the universe." For centuries, unraveling that complexity has been the objective of brain explorers who have dissected animal brains, watched human autopsies, and studied brain wounds and diseases to understand the secrets of the cerebral universe. But until the last decades of the twentieth century, science was still limited in its ability to look inside the brain.

Most of the available techniques required "invading" the brain, or examining it through physical penetration, which could be unsafe. At the same time, such techniques didn't always ensure that conclusions would be scientifically accurate. Research on brain-damaged people didn't necessarily reveal how healthy tissue worked. Nor did autopsies on dead brains give sound answers on live ones. Science still looked for a safe, foolproof window into the brain, one that would let scientists see how the living brain actually functioned.

(Opposite page) Medical researchers continue to develop increasingly sophisticated equipment to view and study the complex machinery of the human brain.

101

That window finally came with advanced technology in the fields of engineering and electronics. Low technology included such primary inventions as the microscope. High technology involves sophisticated computers and other complex tools.

Starting first with the electroencephalograph and moving on to the computer-based brain scanners, high technology let science make a huge leap into "reading" the brain. Computers especially—combined with research in biochemistry, magnetism, and electricity—painted a picture of the brain in all its living glory: three-dimensional, pulsating, and viewable backwards and upside down.

EEG

Experiments with the electrical stimulation of the body in the eighteenth century led to science's first tool for detecting and measuring the electrical energy of the brain, the electroencephalograph (EEG). Research into the brain not only revealed that nerves could be excited by electrical current but could also conduct electricity and, more importantly, could produce small currents on their own.

The next step was to discover a way to measure that current. The first person to make advances in this field was an English physiologist, Richard Caton, in 1875. Using primitive equipment, he placed electrodes on the exposed brain surfaces of animals. His work produced evidence of electrical currents in the brain. This was followed by the discovery that these same voltages could be measured on the outside of the human head without exposing the brain.

The person who made this revelation was German psychiatrist Hans Berger in 1928. Using an apparatus called a galvanometer, he measured

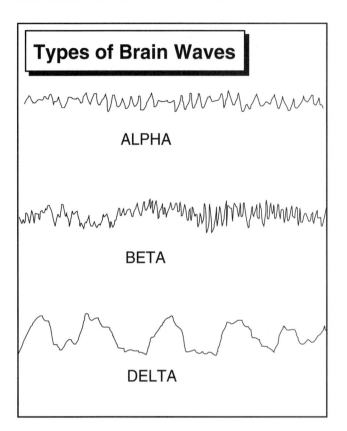

Types of Brain Waves

ALPHA

BETA

DELTA

electrical energy from the skull. As author Anthony Smith says in *The Mind*, "Berger's first reports of a successful recording of rhythmic electrical activity spontaneously generated by the human brain were greeted with incredulity." Skeptics thought that the electricity originated from other sources, not inside the head. But Berger, through other experiments, confirmed his conclusions. The scientific world accepted "Berger rhythms" by 1933 as the four basic rhythms of the brain, identifications which are still used today.

The modern EEG machine works on the same principle as Berger's device. Eight or more wires are selectively attached to spots on a person's scalp. The wires are attached to an amplifier in the EEG machine. Paper revolves around a drum also attached to the EEG. Over the drum are electromagnetic pens. Electrical impulses from the brain via the wires are magnified a million times by the amplifier, marked on the paper by the pens, and graphed as rows of moving waves. The waves are measured by height and frequency (number of waves per second), frequency being the most important criterion in diagnosis.

The traditional EEG machine has been invaluable in determining states of human consciousness, stages of sleep, as well as dreaming and alertness. As a diagnostic tool, it has additionally been important for identifying epileptic seizures or brain damage. That is why, as sleep specialist J. Allan Hobson says in *The Dreaming Brain*, "more than fifty years after Berger's discovery, [it] has become an indispensable tool" in medical diagnosis.

ERP

In the mid-1960s, the high-speed computer took over from the EEG. By computerizing EEGs, science could measure subtle changes in brain activity, how the brain reacts to specific stimulus: the "evoked response potential" (ERP). In reaction to an event like a sound or a flash of light, the brain produces very specific brain waves. An ERP reading first records a variety of EEGs. Then they are computer analyzed; all the EEGs are averaged and the microwave that signals the evoked response is detected. Wiping out the rest of the other EEG "noise," the ERP produces a fine-tuned recording about one-tenth that of regular brain waves.

Evoked response potential testing has been quite valuable in looking for hearing and vision damage in babies, as well as a way to test for learning disorders in children. In other cases, ERP has been used as a diagnostic tool for the comatose, as well as patients suffering from multiple sclerosis, stroke, and brain tumors.

Brain scans

X rays offered one possible route toward achieving this goal. X rays have the capacity to penetrate solid objects without physically invading the body. Scientists wanted to build on the X-ray principle, but overcome its disadvantages: Conventional X rays don't reveal three-dimensional pictures or depth. The first step was the introduction in the 1970s of the world's first brain scanner, the CAT scan. CAT stands for computerized axial tomography. CAT scans project a picture of the brain's structure like a cross-section snapshot, using a computer to reconstruct an image of the brain from many different angles, based on scans from X rays.

To obtain these images a patient lies on a table with his or her head resting in a donut-shaped hole. Around this hole is the special scanner: an X-ray tube that rotates in a circle around the head. The X-ray beams pass through the brain and are absorbed by cerebral tissue of various densities. As the beams are picked up on the rebound, a computer measures the total amount of radiation received and what happened to the X rays. Using this information, it produces a detailed cross-section picture of the brain, projected on a TV screen.

CAT scans are most effective when only still pictures are needed. Rotating around the brain, the device can compare brain tissue densities and pinpoint and determine the growth of a tumor. The medical world has used the CAT on blood clots, birth defects, and brain damage related to senility.

The DSR, or dynamic spatial reconstructor, improved on the CAT. It too is an X-ray machine,

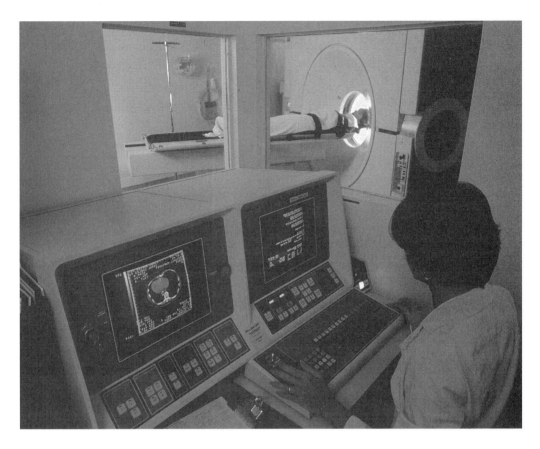

CAT scans reconstruct a three-dimensional image of the brain from many different angles. The scans are so precise they can pinpoint the exact location of a tumor.

but unlike the CAT, the images it reconstructs from X rays are three-dimensional. Developed at the Mayo Clinic in Minnesota and costing $3 million to $5 million apiece, the DSR has qualities which far surpass any previous brain technology. In the same time the CAT takes to make one cross section, the DSR can make seventy-five thousand. Instead of showing just a slice of the brain on a screen, it gives a video panorama: the living, active interior, exposed from different angles.

The DSR creates these images with the aid of twenty-eight separate X-ray guns, circling around the patient and firing sixty times per second. The computer turns the brain into a sophisticated mathematical model. Doctors can actually cut the brain open on the screen, watch blood flow and then manipulate the picture as they wish: replay it, slow it down, or speed it up. In the words of Jack Fincher in *The Brain: Mystery of Matter and Mind*, the DSR is "the most complex and versatile medical instrument ever invented."

PET Scans

But radiology-based technology has taken another turn. In the search for more information about the brain, scientists tapped into a technique in which radioactive substances are actually placed in the body, known as the radioscopic scan. These types of scans have been used by medical science since the 1950s, but until the advent of the computer imaging used in the CAT, the image quality was like watching a very primitive video game.

Biochemistry is their core. These scans monitor chemical activity within the brain, which science now considers to be the brain's main focus. With explosive advances in biochemistry, scientists now realize that the key to understanding the brain lies in learning about its chemistry. To observe that activity, elements called radioactive isotopes are injected in the body. These elements have properties that cause them to disintegrate rapidly. As they decay, they give off radiation, trackable as the isotopes move throughout the body. Following the path of the isotopes gives a diagnosis of disease or activity.

Authors Judith Hooper and Dick Teresi describe the birth of the first computer-based radioscopic scan: the PET scan. "Positron Emission Tomography (PET) was born in 1973 at Washington University in St. Louis, where a scientific team . . . sawed a hole in the center of an old wooden table, fastened radiation detectors around it, and strapped a dog to the platform. The first images were . . . 'funny, squiggley blurs.'" Many improvements later, PET scans were hard at work focusing on the metabolism within the brain.

Metabolism is the rate by which the brain burns glucose (sugar), oxygen, or any other nerve cell–absorbable substances. Unlike most other body tissues, the brain uses separate locations for specialized functions, and metabolizes energy most in response to needs. Richard Restak says: "Measurements of metabolism within the brain provide an indirect indication of what parts of the brain are active at different times." By monitoring where the brain is burning the most glucose, any number of human behaviors, including thoughts and feelings, could be anatomically mapped.

Like CAT and DSR, a patient undergoing a PET scan places his or her head in a scanner. But there is a difference. A glucose solution mixed with a radioactive isotope is first injected into the bloodstream. Isotopes emit atomic particles

Producing colorful images of brain metabolism, the PET is one of the most important tools in the search for more information about the human brain.

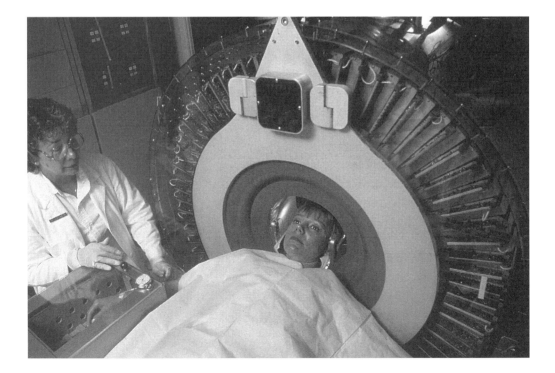

called positrons, or positively charged electrons, which collide with negatively charged electrons in the body. The clash of the two produces radiation, which is then analyzed by a computer, and translated into a pulsating biochemical color picture on a video screen: selected pictures of the living brain over time.

Color enhancement

One major difference between PET and CAT is the use of vivid color. The screens from PET scans shimmer with luminous color. The colors are preselected—cool indigo, for instance, has been selected to highlight low glucose metabolism while crimson is its opposite—and they are not the actual colors of the brain. The colors basically represent radiation counts which have been configured mathematically by the computer into technicolor formulas, representing pictures of the brain that illustrate what brain areas are active. PET images look almost like works of art, yet they are incredible video pictures that pinpoint glucose feeding frenzies inside the brain.

Because the brain is constantly functioning, having only still pictures of the brain does not accurately measure the living brain. The PET overcomes this through dynamic pictures, making the PET one of the most important tools of modern medicine. It has enabled scientists to move beyond what they already know, brain anatomy, and into those areas they do not, what those parts do.

Doctors have used PET to analyze epilepsy, strokes, unsuspected tumors, and such psychiatric conditions as manic depression and schizophrenia. The biggest hope for PET has nothing to do with disease, however. Rather, it's to explore healthy, living brains—and several famous experiments thus far have revealed startling revelations about the abilities of the brain. At UCLA, researchers did a study on whether smart brains worked harder, burning more glucose. Remarkably, it was just the opposite, as Restak says in *The Brain Has a Mind of Its Own.* "Those who performed best on the IQ test tended to produce cooler, more subdued PET scan patterns (blue and green colors), while their less intellectually gifted counterparts lit up like miniature Christmas trees ('hot' red and various orange hues)."

In another part of the world, Dr. Niels Lassen and others at a hospital in Copenhagen, Denmark, were able to obtain the first PET image of human thought. In 1984, a subject in an experiment was told to move his right hand. The image on the PET screen was recorded. Moments later, he was asked just to think about doing this activity. On the PET screen, the brain pattern of thought was unveiled, minus the brain activity that moved his hand. Still another experiment involving music revealed that differences in how the brain processes information make the difference in learning. A musician uses a different part of the brain to listen to music than someone who has no musical background, all of which had implications about brain hemisphere research. Both experiments were historical breakthroughs.

Beyond PET

PET isn't perfect, however. Beyond its multicolored pictures are disadvantages which have spurred the development of other technology. It doesn't measure the brain in "real time," like an EEG, for instance, instead showing brain states every thirty to forty minutes. Nor is it capable of visualizing brain images down to microsize, the millimeter level. Overcoming PET's disadvantages involved visualizing the brain from other points of view. What happened was what *Newsweek* called "an alphabet soup of technologies," each with its advantages and disadvantages.

Sounding like creations from science fiction, each new expensive, computer-based medical imaging device "reads" the brain differently. Magnetic resonance imaging (MRI) uses a powerful magnetic field and radio waves to produce images. Safer than radiology-based technologies, it is more accurate in smaller areas than the PET and can reveal structural brain abnormalities. But MRI cannot detect brain function, and the image it produces is static, not dynamic. The SQUID (superconducting quantum interference device) looks for very small changes in magnetic fields produced by the electric current of firing brain cells. It too shows how the nerve cells are working. Still another, SPECT (single photon emission computerized tomography) focuses on just one sign of activity, blood flow in the brain.

The brain and future technology

Every new piece of brain technology puts one more piece into the giant cerebral puzzle, helping to make the picture clearer. One anticipated type of new, highly reliable technology is actually a throwback to the standard EEG. Called brain electrical activity mapping, or BEAM, it lets science build on the information received from an electroencephalogram. BEAM eliminates the need for a doctor to interpret the brain waves on an EEG recording. It converts the wavy lines into a color-coded map, making the entire reading more visual. A companion technique, significance probability mapping (SPM), shows any EEG deviation from the norm as compared by computer.

Scientists are now talking about ways to combine readings from different technologies to fine-tune accuracy and information. BEAM readings may be used with PET scans, for instance, to ana-

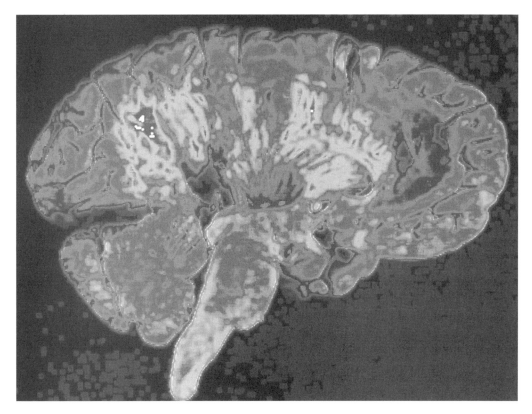

Scientists continue to use images like this brain scan to study the brain in ways once thought impossible.

lyze schizophrenics. Scientists have high hopes, as *Newsweek* says, that they will "stumble upon a Northwest Passage, connections that are totally unexpected, symphonies of neurons that had gone completely unheard."

In just a few short decades, science has gone from having only a few traditional tools to peer into the brain to being armed with sophisticated computers and million-dollar brain scanners capable of detailing the smallest portions of living cerebral tissue. Michael Phelps, the designer of the PET scan, summarized the future of the brain and technology in *The Three-Pound Universe*: "The explosion of knowledge in brain science is equal to our ability to probe outer space. . . . We have the techniques now to probe the inner space of the body."

Through these elaborate, expensive devices that turn the brain into a mathematical model on technicolor TV screens and high-tech gadgets wired intricately to the human head, scientists hope to master the most complex organ in the human body. Predicting diseases, helping to improve intellectual strengths and weaknesses—these are all in the future powers of the brain and technology—including, some say, even the ability to "read the mind." Science is only limited by its imagination.

Glossary

amygdala: An almond-shaped mass in the limbic system thought to control such emotions as rage and aggression.

axon: A long fiber extending from the body of a neuron that transports impulse messages to nearby neurons.

basal ganglia: Four clusters of neurons at the base of the brain that assist in body movements.

brainstem: A series of bulges between the spinal cord and the cerebral hemispheres, consisting of the medulla, pons, and midbrain.

Broca's area: An area within the left frontal lobe that monitors speech production.

cerebellum: A large structure behind the brainstem and above the pons, responsible for coordinating movement.

cerebral cortex: The outer layer of the cerebral hemispheres, wrinkled in appearance; the source of intelligence.

cerebrospinal fluid: A clear fluid located in the ventricles of the brain and spinal canal that helps to cushion the brain.

cerebrum: The biggest and uppermost portion of the brain, composed of the left and right cerebral hemispheres.

corpus callosum: The bridge of nerve fibers that connects the cerebral hemispheres.

Engram: A permanent memory trace in the brain.

ESB: Electrical stimulation of the brain, used to map brain functions.

frontal lobe: The frontmost of the four major divisions of the cortex; the rear of the frontal lobe contains motor functions, but the rest is believed to be responsible for foresight and personality.

hippocampus: A curved formation in the limbic system, thought to play a function in memory.

hypothalamus: A small cluster of nerves at the base of the forebrain; governs such behavior as hormone secretion, sleep, sex, temperature, thirst, and hunger.

limbic system: A group of structures deep in the forebrain involved with emotional behavior.

lobes: The four major sections of the cortex.

neuron: The basic nerve cell of the nervous system. It is composed of the cell body, the axon (a single long fiber that transmits impulses), and the dendrites (shorter extensions that receive impulses).

neurotransmitter: One of at least thirty chemical messengers, released by one neuron, that transmits impulses to another neuron.

NREM sleep: The stages of sleep as it deepens and brain activity and bodily processes decline.

occipital lobe: The lowest section of the cortex, handling vision.

parietal lobe: The middle region of the cortex, between the frontal and occipital lobes; receives information for nerve impulses about touching and orientation.

pineal gland: A small cone-shaped gland at the base of the brain; regulates the body's biological clock.

pituitary gland: Located below the hypothalamus, from which it receives orders, it is the "master gland" for secreting hormones.

REM (rapid eye movement) sleep: The stage of sleep characterized by fluttering eye movements and vivid dreaming.

reticular activating system (also known as the reticular formation or RAS): A web of nerve fibers found in the core of the brainstem; monitors consciousness and focuses attention.

split brain: The surgical separation of the brain into independent left and right cerebral hemispheres.

synapse: The juncture between two neighboring nerve cells across which the chemical neurotransmitters transport nerve impulses.

temporal lobe: The area of the cerebral cortex near the ears, the location for hearing and memory.

thalamus: The relay centers that handle sensory and movement information to and from the brain, positioned at the top of the brainstem.

ventricles: Cavities within the brain filled with cerebrospinal fluid.

Wernicke's area: A specific part of the left hemisphere specialized in the understanding of speech.

Suggestions for Further Reading

W. F. Allman, "Biology of the Mind," *U.S. News & World Report*, December 14, 1992.

S. Begley, "Mapping the Brain," *Newsweek*, April 20, 1992.

Thomas R. Blakesee, *The Right Brain*. Garden City, NY: Doubleday, 1980.

William H. Calvin and George A. Ojemann, *Inside the Brain: Mapping the Cortex, Exploring the Neuron*. New York: The New American Library, 1974.

E. Clark and K. Dewhurst, *An Illustrated History of Brain Function*. Oxford: Sanford Publications, 1972.

Francis Crick and Graeme Mitchison, "The Function of Dream Sleep," *Nature*, July 14, 1983.

Michael Gazzaniga, "The Split Brain in Man," *Scientific American*, August 1967.

Norman Geschwind, "Specializations of the Human Brain," *Scientific American*, September 1979.

A. Gibbons, "New Maps of the Human Brain," *Science*, July 13, 1990.

Erica Goode, "Where Do Emotions Come From?" *U.S. News & World Report*, July 24, 1991.

Stephen LaBerge, "Lucid Dreaming: Directing the Action as It Happens," *Psychology Today*, January 1981.

Melissa Ludtke, "Can the Mind Help Cure Disease?" *Time*, March 12, 1990.

Gina Maranto, "The Mind Within the Brain," *Discover*, May 1984.

J. B. Martin, "Mapping the Human Brain," *Science*, November 20, 1992.

J. M. Nash, "The Frontier Within," *Time* (special edition), Fall 1992.

Richard Restak, *The Brain*. New York: Bantam Books, 1984.

———, *The Brain: The Last Frontier: An Exploration of the Human Mind and Our Future*. New York: Doubleday, 1979.

———, *The Mind*. New York: Bantam, 1988.

Oliver Sacks, *Awakenings*. New York: E. P. Dutton, 1973.

Science News, "Brain Goals for the 1990's," May 8, 1993, p. 303.

Larry Squire, "Memory Highways," *Psychology Today*, May/June 1992.

K. Stein, "Interview: Michael Gazzaniga," *Omni*, October 1993, pp. 99–100.

L. A. Stevens, *Explorers of the Brain*. London: Angus and Robertson, 1973.

Time, "The Right Chemistry," February 15, 1993.

Edith Weart, *The Story of Your Brain and Nerves*. New York: Conrad, McCann, Geoghegan, 1961.

Lee Willerman, "Brains: Is Bigger Better?" *Science*, December 13, 1991.

J. Winston, "The Meaning of Dreams," *Scientific American*, November 1990.

Film

The Brain. John D. and Catherine MacArthur Foundation. Library Video Classics Project. Educational Broadcasting Corporation, 1984.

Works Consulted

Lynn Peters Adler, *Centenarians*. Santa Fe, NM: Health Press, 1995.

William Allman, *Apprentice of Wonder.* New York: Bantam, 1989.

Arthur Ancowitz, *Strokes*. New York: Van Nostrand Reinhold, 1975.

Ronald Bailey and the Editors of Time-Life Books, *The Role of the Brain.* New York: Time-Life Books, 1975.

Richard Bergland, *Fabric of Mind.* New York: Viking, 1985.

Russell Blaylock, *Excitotoxins*. Santa Fe, NM: 1995.

Sue Dauphin, *Parkinson's Disease: The Mystery, the Search, the Promise*. Tequesta, FL: Pixel Press, 1992.

H. Chandler Elliott, *The Shape of Intelligence*. New York: Charles Scribner's Sons, 1969.

Jack Fincher, *The Brain: Mystery of Matter and Mind.* Washington, DC: U.S. News Books, 1981.

Elaine Geralis, ed., *Children with Cerebral Palsy.* Kensington, MD: Woodbine House, 1991.

J. Allan Hobson, *The Dreaming Brain*. New York: Basic Books, 1988.

Judith Hooper and Dick Teresi, *The Three-Pound Universe*. New York: Jeremy Tarcher, 1992.

J. and M. Kastner, *Sleep*. New York: Harcourt Brace, 1968.

Ronald Kotulak, "Unlocking the Mind," *Chicago Tribune*, April 11–15, December 12–15, 1993.

Jack Maguin, *Care and Feeding of the Brain*. New York: Doubleday, 1990.

Alicia Hills Moore, "Technology" section, *Fortune*, December 3, 1990.

Robert Ornstein and Richard Thompson, *Amazing Brain*. Boston: Houghton Mifflin, 1984.

Israel Rosenfield, *The Invention of Memory*. New York: Basic Books, 1988.

Louis Rosner and Shelley Ross, *Multiple Sclerosis*. New York: Simon and Schuster, 1992.

Anthony Smith, *The Mind*. New York: Viking, 1984.

James Wynbrandt, *The Encyclopedia of Genetic Disorders and Birth Defects*. New York: Facts On File, 1991.

Index

About the Author

Jim Barmeier is a native of Chicago. He received a bachelor's degree from Denison University in Ohio and a master's degree from Stanford University in California.

A member of the Writer's Guild of America, he has written several produced episodes of cartoon series including *Smurfs* and *Defenders of the Earth*, created video games, and written jokes for comic Joan Rivers. He currently consults to individuals as president of his own company and lives in the Los Angeles area.

Picture Credits